MANAGING
TO BE
THE BEST

*A Personal
Approach*

W9-DCC-545

MANAGING

TO BE THE BEST

A Personal Approach

MYRON RUSH

WITHDRAWN
by Unity Library

VICTOR BOOKS®

A DIVISION OF SCRIPTURE PRESS PUBLICATIONS INC.
USA CANADA ENGLAND

UNITY SCHOOL LIBRARY
UNITY VILLAGE, MISSOURI 64065

Scripture quotations marked (NIV) are from the *Holy Bible, New International Version,* © 1973, 1978, 1984, International Bible Society. Used by permission of Zondervan Bible Publishers. Verses marked (TLB) are taken from *The Living Bible,* © 1971, Tyndale House Publishers, Wheaton, IL 60189. Used by permission. Quotations marked (PH) are from J.B. Phillips: *The New Testament in Modern English,* Revised Edition, © J.B. Phillips, 1958, 1960, 1972, permission of Macmillan Publishing Co. and Collins Publishers.

Recommended Dewey Decimal Classification: 658
Suggested Subject Heading: MANAGEMENT

Library of Congress Catalog Card Number: 89-60168
ISBN: 0-89693-731-3

© 1989 by SP Publications, Inc. All rights reserved. Printed in the United States of America. No part of this book may be reproduced without written permission, except for brief quotations in books, critical articles, and reviews.

VICTOR BOOKS
A division of SP Publications, Inc.
Wheaton, IL 60187

CONTENTS

Preface 7
1 Decisions That Shape a Manager's Career 9
2 Learning to Handle Success 27
3 How to Manage in the Midst of Change 39
4 Commit to Service as a Lifestyle 51
5 The Role Renewal Plays in Success 63
6 Management Traits That Influence Potential 76
7 Your Management Traits in Action 92
8 Leading vs. Managing 111
9 The Art of Managing Managers 124
10 Training Others to Succeed 138
11 Keeping Your Life in Balance 152
12 God's Plan for Your Career 166

HD
8.2
287
989
.1

PREFACE

Where are you headed in your management career? Do you know what is involved in climbing the organizational ladder? Do you know how to stay at the top once you get there? Where, if any-place, does God fit in your career, and is He concerned about your success?

This book deals with these and other issues you must wrestle with in developing your potential as a manager. In *Management: A Biblical Approach* I dealt more with the "tools" of management. However, in this book we will look more at what you must become as a person to achieve your full management potential.

Principles, by themselves, are of little value unless we act on them. Therefore, you will find personal application assignments at the end of each chapter. These are designed to help you apply the principles presented in each chapter. They also work well as a guideline for small group discussions with other managers or peers.

It is my prayer that this book will be a valuable tool as you pursue the full potential of your management career. I trust that God will use your life and career as a role model of biblical principles effectively at work in the marketplace. May God richly reward and bless you as you faithfully apply His principles in every area of your life.

Myron D. Rush
President, Management Training Systems

1

DECISIONS THAT SHAPE A MANAGER'S CAREER

I first met George Wellermier more than ten years ago when he and his wife, Darlene, visited the church I attended. While looking for a friend's Sunday School class, they wandered into the class I was teaching. When the class was over George introduced himself and his wife and that was the beginning of a long and enjoyable friendship.

One day George called my office and asked if he could buy my lunch. With a laugh he said, "I'm really more interested in talking than eating." So we picked a quiet, little restaurant, had a quick sandwich, and I spent most of the next hour listening to George vent his frustrations about his job.

George worked for a medium-sized manufacturing company. He had been with the firm seven years. During that time he had been promoted three times, and he had spent the last four years as one of the company's production managers.

"I'm getting very bored and frustrated with my job," George said, as he unconsciously tapped the top of the table. "I feel I've learned far more than I need to know to successfully do my job, and I have an excellent record with the company. But frankly, Myron, I'm getting bored, and I know I'm capable of handling a lot more responsibility."

When I asked George if he had talked to his boss and upper management about his feelings, he said, "Oh, several times, including twice last week."

"And what did they say?" I asked, watching him continue tapping the table.

"They told me they really appreciated me and the fine work I had done. They even said I was one of their best managers." He shrugged his shoulders and continued. "It's the same old story every time I talk to them. But the bottom line is there aren't any promotions coming up on the horizon."

George went on to explain that there just wasn't any room for advancement in the foreseeable future. All of the managers and executives above him were very secure in their jobs, and it would be years before any of them would be retiring. It appeared as if he was "locked in" at his present position for quite some time to come.

He smiled and said, "But this time they did offer me a substantial increase in salary, and said in another year they would try to increase my bonus if my department continues to perform at its present rate." Then he looked at me in frustration and said, "Myron, I just don't know what to do. Should I take the nice increase in pay and try to be content where I am, or look for something else outside the company that, while initially a lesser job, will be more challenging and offer more opportunity in the future. What's your advice?"

What would *you* have done in George's situation? Like George, the decision you made would have a great impact on your future career as a manager, as well as on your life. And just like George, that decision would indicate your expectations of potential growth and development as a leader and manager.

Have you decided yet? Many people would choose to take the increase in pay, suppress their desires for more responsibility and the need for a greater challenge, and feel secure in the fact that they are needed and appreciated. They would throttle their desires for more responsibility and the need for a greater challenge. Willing to sacrifice their unused creativity and potential, they would force themselves to be comfortable with the fact that they are standing first in line for the next promotion, even though it may not come for years down the road.

Such people wind up settling for the security of knowing they can do their job very well, and content themselves with the fact that they are being paid a good salary. What about you? What decision would you make? One by one, the decisions we make during the course of each day are helping mold, shape, and determine our future.

THE OBJECTIVE OF THIS BOOK

In *Management: A Biblical Approach* (Victor Books, 1983), I described how to manage people and organizations using proven biblical principles. The book examines the enormous difference between the secular and biblical viewpoints. It presents the fundamentals of management from a biblical perspective: planning, decision-making, communication, team building, performance evaluation, and problem-solving.

This follow-up book incorporates a similar biblical framework. However, it goes beyond the presentation and discussion of basic "tools of the trade" and, in addition, discusses the manager as a *person*, presenting the qualities, traits, and characteristics required for managerial success.

Besides discussing "what to do as a manager," this book also deals with what and who you are as a leader and manager. It shows that the person you are has a profound impact on what you do, or don't do, when managing businesses and organizations. My goal is to help you cultivate the personal qualities necessary in developing your full potential as a manager.

Like *Management: A Biblical Approach,* this book also contains "personal application projects" at the end of each chapter. Study each one carefully and apply them enthusiastically. The purpose of this book is to help you *be* a good manager, not to just know what good managers do. Therefore, it is important to apply what you learn. The aim of this book is more practical than philosophical.

A friend of mine, a former personnel director of a regional federal agency, once told me, "Myron, I'm sick and tired of sending our managers and supervisors off for training that doesn't produce results on the job!" After grumbling about the thousands of dollars his agency spent each year on ineffective training and development programs, he said, "Most management training seminars are becoming nothing more than spray and pray sessions! We spray people with sophisticated, hypothetical management philosophy floating in alphabet soup terminology and pray that some of it works!"

Unfortunately, my friend's words are too true. Many would-be management consultants and so-called training specialists only tend to add confusion to frustration. They preach grandiose theories and philosophies, conceived in ivory towers, but when they are applied to the cold, hard realities of business, many of these theories prove to be at best impractical, and frequently totally unworkable.

That is why I get so excited about biblical principles of management. The Bible is much more than just a book on the spiritual dimension of man. It is a textbook on how to live life. As a businessman I have discovered that the organizational and management principles presented in Scripture are more relevant and practical than those I've found anywhere else.

In fact, most of the best business and management principles being practiced today can be traced directly to the Bible. Many people using these principles aren't aware that they were instituted by God and successfully used and applied by people thousands of years ago in a variety of different cultures. The biblical principles of management presented are just as relevant, practical, and applicable today as they were when they were first written.

However, these time-tested and proven principles are of no value unless applied. Therefore, I strongly urge you not to just read this book, but to make a commitment to applying the principles of leadership and management contained on its pages. In so doing you will discover the keys to developing your full potential as a manager.

PROMOTE YOUR MANAGEMENT CAREER

People don't reach their full potential as managers simply because they were born with natural ability, but because they are willing to make the necessary decisions to develop their abilities. There is much more involved in developing your management potential than effectively establishing management functions such as: planning, organizing, leading, evaluating, and controlling. Many people are excellent planners, but never progress beyond the level of a first line supervisor. Others are highly organized and efficient, but never achieve their goals of progressing in their management career.

It takes much more than basic management skill to reach your full potential. Even though it is extremely important to have mastered the basic tools of management, there are specific decisions that must be made and committed to for an individual to develop his or her full potential in a management career. The highly successful manager will not only make these decisions, but will encourage employees and peers to make them as well.

In order to develop your management potential you must decide to:

- Be a learner.
- Seek more responsibility.
- Avoid the "settle for" mentality.
- Focus on "the big picture."
- Be a trainer, not just a manager.
- Develop and maintain balance in your life.
- Always make it on your own merits.
- Commit to applying biblical standards of personal ethics.

If you are interested in increasing your capacity as a manager, it is imperative that you make these important decisions and carry them out on a daily basis. As you do, you will discover you are not only increasing your capacity as a manager, but in other areas of your life as well. There are many factors that are involved in reaching your full potential in management. Regardless of what you have been led to believe, you are in control of most, if not all, of them. It is extremely difficult, if not impossible, to develop your managerial potential unless you incorporate these eight decisions into your life on an ongoing basis.

These are not one time decisions to make and then forget about. They are decisions that, when applied daily, help you develop a way of life that will propel you along the path of your potential. When applied collectively and consistently, these eight decisions will prove more valuable in helping you reach your management potential than all your professional degrees.

BE A LEARNER

When I had lunch with George Wellermier, I asked him what job he had started out with in the company. He laughed and said, "I started out in inventory control. My job was to help keep track of everything coming in and going out."

George quickly discovered that he didn't want to do that job the rest of his life. "Once I had mastered my job I began looking around in the company to see what I'd really like to do," he said. "It didn't take me long to figure out that there wasn't much of a future in keeping track of nuts and bolts."

George decided he would like to transfer to sales. He had met some of the sales "reps" in the lunchroom and thought they had much more interesting and exciting jobs. "They made a lot more money than I was making," he chuckled. "However, they also told me the company hired only people with sales experience, and the only person I had ever been able to sell anything to was Darlene when I convinced her to marry me!"

However, George was determined to better his situation. After talking to some of the salespeople, George realized he knew more about their products than many of them did. Working in inventory control had given him the opportunity not only to learn about the products his company manufactured and sold, but about the components going into those products as well.

"Once I decided I wanted to transfer into sales, I learned everything I could about our products, and the competition's as well," George said. "I kept talking to the salespeople and I started reading every book on sales I could find. I even drove to hear one of those high-powered sales motivators speak." He laughed and continued, "I'm sure I was the only inventory-control type in the whole room! But I didn't care. I was there to learn everything I could about how to be a successful salesman."

George's commitment to become a successful salesman paid off. He was the first person the company hired in sales who didn't have selling experience. "Once I got into sales I kept right on learning," George said. "I was committed to being the best salesperson in the company."

George's move to being a production manager came about in the same way. "I soon realized I wanted to get more involved in the company. Even though I enjoyed sales, made good money, and learned a lot, I really wanted to be more involved in decision-making, where I perceived the real action was—the manufacturing of the product. So I made my move."

George began learning everything about how the product was made. He talked to people on the assembly line and to supervisors in the production area. He got acquainted with some of the engineers and started reading the trade journals that were scattered around the meeting rooms and offices.

"My first job in manufacturing was supervising assembly lines," George said. "At that time I realized I knew more about our business and its products than a lot of the supervisors and managers who had been around for years. I discovered the importance of my decision to learn about the company's products. People started coming to me with their questions. I was asked to sit in on meetings that other supervisors weren't invited to attend. I kept learning everything I could, not only about my job, but about other departments as well. And when Frank Roseman, the production manager, retired four years ago they offered me his job." Beaming with pride, George said, "I was the youngest department manager in the entire company."

"To learn, you must want to be taught. To refuse reproof is stupid" (Prov. 12:1, TLB). And verse 15 of the same chapter says, "A fool thinks he needs no advice, but a wise man listens to others." If you want to advance in your management career, be a learner. As Proverbs 12:1 points out, before you can learn you must first be willing to be taught. Are you willing to be taught? Do you feel you know how to do your job and don't need to learn from others? If so, you will have a hard time making the decision to become a learner.

If you want to advance in your management career, be a learner. Learn everything you can, not only about your own job, but about other jobs and departments within the organization as well. As you do, you will discover, like George did, that people will begin seeking you out for your opinions and answers to their problems. In the process of sharing what you have learned with others, you will earn the right to handle more and more responsibility.

The decision to become a learner is one of the most important ones you can make as a leader and manager. However, don't just strive to acquire knowledge, but put into practice what you learn—make no mistake, for only then will you begin developing your potential as a manager and a person.

Learn from your mistakes and failures. We all make mistakes and fail from time to time. Failure can be one of life's very best teachers if we are open to learning and willing to accept constructive criticism. When you fail, learn everything you can concerning why you failed. Seek out other people who have dealt with the same situation and ask for their opinions and advice.

Proverbs 15:31-32 tells us, "If you profit from constructive criticism you will be elected to the wise men's hall of fame. But to reject criticism is to harm yourself and your own best interests" (TLB). Wise people invite constructive criticism and learn everything they can from their mistakes and failures. During my first job as a manager I decided, that if at all possible, I would not make the same mistake twice. I kept a notebook in my desk drawer, and every time I made a major mistake or experienced a failure, I would record what happened, why I failed, and what should be done to avoid such problems in the future. What I learned from those notes was far more important and beneficial to me than any MBA degree.

SEEK MORE RESPONSIBILITY

I have always hated traditional job descriptions. It has been my experience that managers look at a job description one of two ways (and how they view it tells you a lot about that manager's level of motivation). We either look at the job description as a document that *requires* us to take action, or *prevents* us from taking action.

And if you are interested in advancing your management career, learn all you can about your job and organization, and then make a decision to diligently seek more responsibility than is outlined in your present job description. There are basically two kinds of managers—those who *make things happen,* and *those who watch things happen.*

Those who make things happen generally assume they have all the authority they need to properly do the job, and continue to aggressively assume and use their power until those above them say, "Your authority ends here." On the other hand, those who watch things happen usually are very concerned about where their authority begins and ends, and frequently fail to take action because they are uncertain about their authority to do so.

The Book of Nehemiah in the Old Testament has always been one of my favorite books. I have developed a great deal of respect for Nehemiah as a manager. Nehemiah was a man who made his mark on the pages of Bible history, and became a great manager and leader, because he was willing to seek more responsibility than his present job description called for.

In chapter one of the book that bears his name we learn that Nehemiah was an Israelite slave and the personal cupbearer to the Persian king, Artaxerxes. As cupbearer, Nehemiah's job was to taste the king's drinks first to make sure they didn't contain poison. His job description in no way prepared him to become an effective manager.

Nehemiah was a lowly slave whose life was considered totally expendable by the king. However, Nehemiah was destined for greatness, not because he was the king's cupbearer, but because he was willing to seek more responsibility than his present job called for. From fellow Israelite slaves Nehemiah learned that the city of Jerusalem was in ruin. The walls of the city had been torn down and many of the buildings destroyed.

Nehemiah went to the king and asked for the authority to go to Jerusalem and organize and supervise the rebuilding of the city's wall and buildings. Notice his bold request to the king, "If it pleases the king and if your servant has found favor in his sight, let him send me to the city in Judah where my fathers are buried so that I can rebuild it" (Neh. 2:5, NIV).

Nehemiah must have been doing a good job as the king's cupbearer, because when this slave asked for a great deal more responsibility, his master, the king, granted the request. The king undoubtedly had many other Israelite slaves working for him, but Nehemiah got the job because he had made a decision to seek more responsibility. Nehemiah was given a great deal of authority and backing from the king, and was able to organize and motivate a work force to rebuild the wall of Jerusalem in a record time of only fifty-two days (Neh. 6:15).

As I read the Book of Nehemiah, I am greatly impressed with this man's managerial and leadership skills. He was in charge of the entire restoration project, and yet he had been a lowly cup-bearer. He reached the top in management, in part, because of his willingness to seek more responsibility when he saw a need to be met and a project that needed to be done. And like Nehemiah, you too can assist in the development of your management career by seeking more responsibility once you have learned to do your present job well.

Nehemiah serves as a lasting testimony that where one starts out in life has nothing to do with how far one can go. However, as Nehemiah proved, you can reach the top in a management career if you are only willing to step out and seek more responsibility, and then do your work well.

During my discussion with George Wellermier he said, "I know a lot of people were upset when I was promoted to production manager because they felt they should have had the job. But I was the one always looking for more things to do, not they." George explained that as soon as he felt comfortable as assembly-line supervisor he went to his boss and told him he would like to learn about production scheduling. Next he went to the personnel department and had the company's personnel policies and procedures thoroughly explained to him.

"No one in production correctly understood the company's complicated vacation eligibility schedule for new employees, so I went directly to the personnel department and had them explain the policies and procedures." He chuckled and said, "Before I learned how to interpret the policies, every supervisor, including our manager, sent everyone with a personnel question to that department for the answer. However, before long I was the personnel office's unofficial representative for the entire production department."

It was obvious why George became the youngest manager in the entire company. He may not have been the smartest person in line for the job, and he certainly hadn't been with the company as long as many of his peers, but he was committed to learning all that he could, and seeking more responsibility to develop as a manager/leader.

If you want to develop your management potential, don't sit around and wait for the organization to hand you a promotion. Do your current job to the best of your ability and then actively seek more responsibility. Many managers complain about not getting promotions, but are doing nothing to show their superiors that they are ready to handle the greater responsibilities that usually accompany a promotion. On the other hand, those employees who learn all they can about their job and the organization and actively seek more responsibility are almost always the first to be promoted when advancements are available.

AVOID THE "SETTLE FOR" MENTALITY

Earlier in the chapter I asked you what you would do if you were in George Wellermier's position. George appeared to be locked into his job as production manager. He had been doing the job for four years and was interested in a promotion, but no opportunity for advancement was available in the near future. However, George had been offered a considerable increase in pay and the possibility of an increase in his yearly bonus. He was trying to decide whether to stay with the company or move on to another firm where the money might not be as good to start, but the opportunity for advancement would be greater. How would you decide?

George decided to start looking for a job that would provide greater opportunity for advancement. He took a job as production supervisor with a firm on the West Coast. He said, "It's really a demotion, but they are a very progressive company, and I'm actually supervising more people and have more responsibility than I had as production manager with my old job."

Many of his friends told him he was crazy to make the move. They couldn't understand why he would be willing to take less pay and a lesser position. They questioned why he would leave a familiar area and the friends he and his family had made. However, I knew why George had left. He wasn't willing to "settle for" good pay and job security when he knew he was capable of making a much greater contribution somewhere else.

The "settle for" mentality keeps a lot of managers from developing their potential and accomplishing the things of which they are capable. Like the old saying, "A bird in the hand is worth two in the bush," many managers are all too willing to settle for the security of what they have, rather than run the risk involved in making a move. This can lead to complacency.

If George had settled for the security of what he had, in all probability, he would still be production manager in his old job, frustrated and bored because he wasn't performing up to his potential. George didn't have a "settle for" mentality. He took a different job in another firm. Yes, he had to take a demotion and less pay to begin with, but today George is one of the vice presidents of the firm and is thoroughly enjoying his job.

Nehemiah could have settled for his position as the king's cupbearer. After all, he had it a lot better than some of the Israelite slaves. He got to be in the king's court. He had good food and shelter. Things could have been a lot worse. But Nehemiah didn't have a "settle-for" mentality either. He was willing to seek more responsibility. He was willing to run the risks involved in going to his homeland to restore the city of Jerusalem. Because they avoided the "settle-for" mentality, both Nehemiah and George Wellermier were able to help promote their careers as managers.

What about you, have you decided yet? Are you willing to avoid the "settle-for" mentality in order to help develop your skills and abilities as a manager? The choice is up to you. But I can assure you, if you want to reach your full potential as a manager you must avoid the "settle-for" mentality at all costs.

Before continuing I would like to speak frankly to the business owner or executive who may have a "George Wellermier" working in your business or organization. I have just challenged the manager to avoid the "settle-for" mentality. And now I want to challenge you to make every effort to find a place in your business or organization for the supervisor or manager who is willing to be a learner and seek more responsibility.

Sit down with that employee and revamp his or her job description if necessary and provide the challenge that employee needs to feel fulfilled in the job. However, a word of caution is needed. Don't create fancy titles or meaningless positions in an effort to keep such people. Give the employee the opportunity to be creative, even if it means stepping out into an area totally new and different for you and the business or organization. Remember, the effective executive molds his or her organization around the talents, skills, and capacities of the employees instead of forcing the employees into the rigid structure of the organizational chart. And if you aren't willing to create the flexibility necessary to keep a person like George Wellermier, does your business or organization really deserve such a person anyway?

FOCUS ON "THE BIG PICTURE"

I will never forget the advice I received in starting my first business. An elderly gentleman in our church, a retired businessman, took me aside and said, "Young man, if you're going to make it in your own business you've got to focus on the big picture."

His name was Ernest Rainer, and when I asked him to explain what he meant by that statement he continued. "You have to learn that accounting is just as important as sales, and service is just as important as the product you sell. In other words, you have to be able to realize the important role each facet of your business plays—focus on the big picture, boy!"

As a manager it is easy to get tunnel vision. It is easy to get wrapped up in your own job or department and lose sight of what is happening in the rest of the organization. To grow with the organization you first must enlarge your vision of the business or organization's various functions. And for most of us, this does not come naturally. We must work at it.

If you are a supervisor in the accounting department, your primary concern is the function and smooth operation of the accounting process. However, it is easy to get so involved in the processes of your own job or department that you lose sight of the organization's overall objectives. When that happens you may be tempted to start looking at people in other departments as problems in the way of your getting your job done. Such thinking is a sign of immaturity on the supervisor's part. To develop as a manager, you first must begin looking at the organization as a whole and not just your department.

Begin focusing on the overall needs of the organization and what is best for the achievement of its goals. Broaden your vision. Develop interest and concern for what is going on elsewhere in other divisions and departments. Realize that other people and departments play just as important a role as you. Be as concerned for the needs and problems of others as you are for your own.

If your goal is to become a general manager someday, begin looking at the organization from the general manager's point of view. I assure you the view is quite different from his office than it is from the first line supervisor's station. Your ability to develop and advance in your career as a manager will be in direct proportion to your willingness and ability to focus on the big picture, and what the entire organization is attempting to accomplish.

BE A TRAINER, NOT JUST A MANAGER

There are lots of good managers in organizations today, but very few managers are also good trainers. In my book, *The New Leader* (Victor Books, 1987), I pointed out how important it is for leaders to be able to train others to do their jobs.

One of the best ways to help acquire a promotion for yourself is to have someone trained to take your place. Being able to train others in what you do as a manager is essential for reaching your full potential as a manager. Therefore, don't simply focus on the task of managing the department or division; make a decision and commitment to train your subordinates to manage as well. As you train others you will discover increasing opportunities for advancement in your own career.

DEVELOP AND MAINTAIN BALANCE IN YOUR LIFE

Without balance in your life you are a prime candidate for burnout. I went through severe burnout a few years ago because my life was out of balance, and it cost me my family, a business, and a great deal of emotional pain that could have been avoided.

The higher you go in the management profession the more pressures and problems you must face. These pressures and problems can lead to burnout if your life gets out of balance. Most managers know how to work, but few know what to do with the rest of their lives. As a result, it is easy for the manager's job to become his whole life. This is extremely unhealthy. You *must* learn how to balance your work with other activities, especially if you are interested in staying at the top once you get there!

ALWAYS MAKE IT ON YOUR OWN MERITS

Proverbs 22:16 tells us, "He who gains by oppressing the poor or by bribing the rich shall end in poverty" (TLB). This verse is teaching a very important principle. We should neither take advantage of those weaker than us, or try to buy the favor of those stronger. We should make it through life on our own merits. And that certainly applies to the manager as he works at progressing in his career.

Never step on others on your way up the career ladder. If your supervisors are going to be impressed with you, let them be fascinated with the fact that you aren't trying to impress them, but are simply doing your best job. Proverbs 27:2 states, "Don't praise yourself; let others do it!" (TLB) You will advance farther in your career by letting others praise what you do, than by trying to impress your superiors.

As you scale the ladder, make it on your own merits; then you will not be burdened by political debts or favors owed. The interest charged on such political debts and favors is far greater than the value of the original "loan." The philosophy, "Owe no man anything," applies as you develop your career as a manager. I can't stress enough the importance of making it on your own merits. You may have to work harder getting to the top, but that is a small price to pay compared to the burdens accumulated in playing the organization's political game of "favoritism."

APPLYING BIBLICAL PERSONAL ETHICS

Of all the traits you can incorporate into your life, the commitment to apply biblical personal ethics is by far the most important. According to Proverbs 21:3, "God is more pleased when we are just and fair than when we give Him gifts" (TLB). And Proverbs 16:11 states, "The Lord demands fairness in every business deal. He established this principle" (TLB).

To promote your management career, make sure you become known as a person who demands fairness in all your dealings with subordinates, peers, superiors, clients, and customers. That decision must become the foundation on which you develop your management actions, decisions, and practices.

Notice what Matthew 7:12 tells us, "In everything, do to others what you would have them do to you, for this sums up the Law and the Prophets" (NIV). If you commit to applying the principle of that verse, you will insure that you are always treating others just and fair.

Being just and fair is not always popular in today's organizational arena. You may be asked to compromise what you know is right. You may be asked to look the other way when wrongdoing is committed. However, you must never compromise biblical standards, even if your peers ridicule you for your stand. Remember, it is much more important to please God than man.

Make a commitment to applying these eight decisions for promoting your management career. Make them a part of your life as you go to work each day, and challenge your peers and subordinates to incorporate them into their lives. People and organizations that emphasize these eight decisions will be well on their way to developing their God-given potential.

IS IT WRONG TO WANT TO REACH THE TOP?

During management seminars I am frequently asked, "Is it wrong to want to reach the top in my profession?" The answer is no. In 1 Timothy 3:1 we are told, "Here is a trustworthy saying: If anyone sets his heart on being an overseer, he desires a noble task" (NIV).

I realize this verse is speaking about spiritual leadership, but I believe the principle also applies to the business world as well. For example, Proverbs 22:29 states, "Do you know a hard-working man? He shall be successful and stand before kings!" (TLB) God seems to be pointing out that there is a reward called success for hard work, and such people will be found at the top of society's organizational structure.

Jesus describes the responsibility that accompanies climbing the organizational ladder: "Among the heathen, kings are tyrants and each minor official lords it over those beneath him. But among you it is different. Anyone wanting to be a leader among you must be your servant. And if you want to be right at the top, you must serve like a slave. Your attitude must be like My own, for I, the Messiah, did not come to be served, but to serve, and to give My life as a ransom for many" (Matt. 20:25-28, TLB).

First of all, notice that Jesus seems not to condemn climbing the career ladder. However, he points out that Christians are told not to use the power and authority that go with their positions to "lord it over people" the way the rest of the world does. The Christian leader/manager has the responsibility of using the authority of his position to serve those under and around him.

Therefore, our motive for wanting to climb the organizational ladder should be service to those around us, not service of our own interests. Yes, it's OK to reach for the top, but the further up the career ladder we go, the greater our responsibility to those under us. So strive to reach your potential as a leader and manager, not simply to fulfill your own interests and ego, but so that we can have more models of biblical management in the marketplace.

Today, as never before, we need men and women in the marketplaces of the world who will stand upon biblical principles in their professional lives. Regardless of the world's actions, we Christians in leadership and management positions need to be committed to applying God's principles in our day-to-day activities. If our peers in the marketplace are ever going to become interested in following the ways of God, they will do so because of our example.

Every day we are witnesses in the marketplace for Jesus Christ; the question is, are we good witnesses or poor ones? Jesus tells us that we should let our light shine before others in ways that attract them to God. Are people attracted to God because of the way you lead and manage within your business or organization? They should be.

PERSONAL APPLICATION

1. What are your career goals as a manager or leader? If you don't have those goals clearly defined, spend time thinking and praying about them. Write them out and review them each week.
2. Review the eight decisions that promote your management career:
   a. Identify those decisions in which you are the strongest and weakest.
   b. Develop a personal action plan for more effectively imple-

menting each of the eight decisions.
3. Study Matthew 20:25-28. How will you begin to more effectively serve the needs of those people you lead and manage?
4. Read Matthew 5:13-16.
   a. How effective do you feel you have been in letting your light shine in the marketplace?
   b. According to this passage, what should our actions as leaders and managers cause people to do?
   c. How can you become a more effective witness for Jesus Christ on your job?
5. How will you use the principles in this chapter to better develop your management and leadership skills?

2

LEARNING TO HANDLE SUCCESS

I was raised deep in the "blackjack" hills of central Oklahoma on a small, forty-acre farm on which we unsuccessfully attempted to raise cotton. We, along with everyone else in this rural, backwoods area known as Sandyland, were very poor. Between cotton crops, sometimes so bad they didn't even pay for the seed needed to plant the next year's crop, we survived by taking eggs and cream to the little country town each week and selling them for necessities we couldn't produce on our little farm.

The only social functions in that poverty-stricken community were church activities or gatherings at neighbors' houses where we talked about the events of our world, which only extended a few miles down the narrow dirt roads in either direction.

I still have very fond and vivid memories of those childhood years, especially the times sitting and listening to the adults talk about all the things grown-ups know and discuss. But what I remember most about those times is the advice my dad used to give me. He used to say, "Son, if you're ever going to get ahead in this world when you grow up, leave this part of the country. Don't do what I did. Get an education, save your money, and start your own business—that's the only way you'll ever get ahead in life."

My father told me that many times while I was growing up on that poor, red-dirt farm. I grew up believing him. My older sister was the first person in my family to go to college. My parents scrimped and saved for years in order for her to go off to school. And when she got out of college she helped pay for my education. I took my father's advice to heart. I worked hard, saved my money, and the year he died I started my first business.

Recently, for the first time since my father died, I returned to visit the rural community where I spent the first few years of my childhood. I was shocked to find out how little things had changed. For the most part, our space-age world, swimming in the rapidly changing currents of high technology, has completely bypassed that little island of past history.

However, I had changed. I had left this simple world where time seemed to have stood still. I had eagerly waded into the mainstream of our modern day society where fortune hunters frequently exhaust themselves in their struggle to achieve success.

THE LAND OF OPPORTUNITY

More than any other country in the world, ours is a land of abundant opportunity. Very few countries in the world provide both the freedoms and opportunities that enable our citizens to climb out of the depths and despair of poverty and up the so-called "ladder of success." Ours has truly been a land "flowing with milk and honey." As a result, many Americans are gorging themselves off the fat of the land.

Unfortunately, our insatiable appetites for more of the things only money can buy has created a modern American society that feeds on material possessions. We have become a nation addicted to "the good life"; we cannot get enough of what it has to offer. In the process we are slowly, but surely, destroying ourselves.

Things that yesterday were considered "luxuries" today are viewed as absolute necessities. We not only want and believe we need *more*; we have deceived ourselves into believing we must have it *now!* And many of us are willing to do almost anything it takes to get it.

DEFINING TRUE SUCCESS

Recently I was asked to speak at a Christian businessmen's banquet. There, I was introduced to a tall, well-dressed, elderly gentleman with silver-white hair—Damon Franklin, the president of the group.

Mr. Franklin was one of the wealthiest and most successful businessmen in the city. I learned of large commercial develop-

28

ments Mr. Franklin had either built or in which he owned considerable interest.

Damon was a very pleasant, gracious, and humble man. We were enjoying getting acquainted when a young man, probably in his mid-twenties, approached and said, "Mr. Franklin, I'm a reporter for the local newspaper, and I wondered if you would mind if I asked you a few questions before the banquet starts."

If Damon was annoyed he covered his feelings well. He smiled, introduced me to the reporter, and said, "What can I do for you?"

The young business reporter explained that he was preparing an article on businesspeople and personal success. "What do you feel is the secret to your success?" he asked, holding a small microphone in front of Mr. Franklin.

Damon studied the young man very carefully for a moment and then replied. "What makes you think I'm so successful?" he questioned the young man.

The reporter straightened up, and with a surprised look on his face stammered, "Why, sir, because you are . . . because you have acquired a great deal as a businessman."

Mr. Franklin continued to carefully study the young man and said, "Do you mean to say you consider me to be a success because I've acquired a great deal of money, possessions, and wealth during my career as a businessman?"

The young reporter smiled and said, "Why, yes sir! I guess that is exactly what I meant—sir."

For the next few minutes Damon Franklin presented one of the best dissertations on "success" I have ever heard. He calmly and very graciously explained that the amount of wealth and possessions one was able to acquire had absolutely nothing to do with success or failure. He said, "The wife of one of my very dear friends divorced him last year because of his drinking, and he committed suicide just this past week. He had more wealth and possessions than I do. Was he a successful man?"

The reporter was speechless. Damon smiled and continued. "He was able to amass a large fortune, but I certainly wouldn't say his life was a success, would you?" He kept pressing the young man for a response.

Finally the reporter managed a weak smile, nodded, and said, "I guess I see your point," and putting his microphone away, excused himself and slowly walked away.

What is your definition of success? We live in a society that has gone success mad. There are books that tell us how to dress for success, how to be successful playing tennis or golf, how to succeed in buying and selling real estate, how to take a successful vacation, and even books on how to be a success at sex! But what is success? How would you define this mania that has gripped our society?

Before defining true success I want to emphasize the importance of your definition in shaping your managerial career. Your view of success will greatly influence not only the *way* you manage and lead people, but *why* you want to climb the management career ladder.

The world's view of success is far different from God's. The world tends to equate success with possessions and accomplishments. From the world's vantage point, success is always measured by the amount you are able to achieve, perform, or accomplish. However, God's view of success goes far beyond the world's view, encompassing what you are spiritually.

Notice what Revelation 3:17-19 tells us:

You say, "I am rich, with everything I want; I don't need a thing!" And you don't realize that spiritually you are wretched and miserable and poor and blind and naked. My advice to you is to buy pure gold from Me, gold purified by fire—only then will you truly be rich. And to purchase from Me white garments, clean and pure, so you won't be naked and ashamed; and to get medicine from Me to heal your eyes and give you back your sight. I continually discipline and punish everyone I love; so I must punish you, unless you turn from your indifference and become enthusiastic about the things of God (TLB).

The world seeks success to become independent and self-secure. Our independence and self-security tempts us to become indifferent toward God because success frequently deceives us into believing we no longer need God.

Such thinking is very dangerous. Notice again what God says in the first part of this passage. "You say, 'I am rich, with everything I want; I don't need a thing!' " That certainly is the attitude of many people once they acquire "success."

However, notice what God says next. "And you don't realize that spiritually you are wretched and miserable and poor and blind and naked." Worldly success tends to deceive and blind us spiritually. Material success frequently leads to a lack of worry about our spiritual development and success.

God goes on to say, "My advice to you is to buy pure gold from Me, gold purified by fire—only then will you truly be rich." The Lord is telling us that true riches and success come only through our spiritual development and relationship with Him. And if we refuse to develop our spiritual relationship with Him, God says, "I must punish you, unless you turn from your indifference and become enthusiastic about the things of God."

True success is *the progressive realization of a worthwhile goal, which is only fully achieved when we focus on our spiritual development, as well as on our personal accomplishments.*

SUCCESS VS. HAPPINESS

Many people make the mistake of believing that worldly success is synonymous with happiness. They are convinced that if you are successful according to society's standards you will also be happy. As a result, the majority of people seek happiness through success. Believing that success is measured by possessions and accomplishments, they wind up seeking happiness through these things.

According to society's standards, Damon Franklin's friend, who committed suicide, was a successful man. He had accumulated a great deal of wealth and possessions, yet he obviously wasn't happy.

I recently heard a sports announcer state that he couldn't understand why a noted professional athlete had allowed his career to be destroyed by drugs. He said, "He had everything going for himself. He had all the money he needed, fame, and a nice family. I just don't understand how such a thing can happen to someone like that!"

The sports announcer, like so many people in society today, was assuming that material possessions and success produce happiness. However, that certainly is not the case. Notice how the Book

31

of Ecclesiastes describes people who try to find happiness in success as defined by society:

I undertook great projects: I built houses for myself and planted vineyards. I made gardens and parks and planted all kinds of fruit trees in them. I made reservoirs to water groves of flourishing trees. I bought male and female slaves and had other slaves who were born in my house. I also owned more herds and flocks than anyone else in Jerusalem before me. I amassed silver and gold for myself. . . . I acquired men and women singers, and a harem as well—the delights of the heart of man. I became greater by far than anyone in Jerusalem before me. . . . I denied myself nothing my eyes desired; I refused my heart no pleasure. . . . Yet when I surveyed all that my hands had done and what I had toiled to achieve, everything was meaningless, a chasing after the wind (Ecc. 2:4-11, NIV).

The Preacher clearly illustrates how futile it is to try to find happiness through "things." Elsewhere, the Bible tells us the source of true happiness: "What happiness for those whose guilt has been forgiven! What joys when sins are covered over! What relief for those who have confessed their sins and God has cleared their record" (Ps. 32:1-2, TLB).

True happiness comes as a result of being in right relationship to God. Observe what Psalm 119:1-2 states: "Happy are all who perfectly follow the laws of God. Happy are all who search for God, and always do His will" (TLB).

Happiness can never be found in striving for wordly success; it comes only as we ask God to forgive our sins and follow His will for our lives. This is a foundational truth to learn as you develop and promote your management career.

TEMPTATIONS THAT COME WITH SUCCESS

Every manager climbing the organizational ladder must face the success issue. And the further up the ladder you go, the more you must deal with the temptations that come with success. These temptations become more and more serious, and have much broader ramifications the more successful you become.

The successful manager, like any other person, faces all sorts of temptations. However, the following four are the most serious for the Christian manager/leader:

1. *To start taking the credit for your success.* This is one of the first ways Satan attacks the Christian manager/leader progressing in a management career. Deuteronomy 8:10-18 provides a clear warning against taking the credit for what God allows us to do:

> When you have eaten and are satisfied, praise the Lord your God for the good land He has given you. Be careful that you do not forget the Lord your God. . . . Otherwise, when you eat and are satisfied, when you build fine houses and settle down, and when your herds and flocks grow large and your silver and gold increases . . . then your heart will become proud and you will forget the Lord your God. . . . You may say to yourself, "My power and the strength of my hands have produced this wealth for me." But remember the Lord your God, for it is He who gives you the ability to produce wealth (Deut. 8:10-18, NIV).

This passage shows us how easy it is to start taking the credit for the accomplishments and successes we have as leaders. Notice verse 10 says, "When you have eaten and are satisfied, praise the Lord your God for the good land He has given you." We can ward off the temptation to take credit for our accomplishments by praising God and giving Him the credit He deserves. Praising God takes the focus and attention away from ourselves and places it where it should be.

In 2 Corinthians 11:30 Paul warns about bragging over our successes and accomplishments saying, "If I must boast, I will boast of the things that show my weakness" (NIV). Paul isn't encouraging us to run ourselves down and focus on the negative. He is simply pointing out that we need to realize the poverty in such boasting.

Avoid the temptation of giving yourself credit for your success. God deserves the credit, not us, because He is the source of all our success and accomplishments. Therefore, if we want to boast, we should boast "in the Lord." After all, He is the one who deserves the credit.

2. *To stop trusting God.* As we continue to develop and increase our management skills, the next major temptation Satan throws at us is to forget the Lord. We get very comfortable with our position, abilities, and successes. At that point it is easy to

begin thinking that we have the answers. We have dealt with these problems and situations before and we know what to do and how to do it. The temptation is to start trusting in our own abilities and stop trusting God for help and guidance.

Remember the error of Rehoboam. "After Rehoboam's position as king was established and he had become strong, he and all Israel with him abandoned the law of the Lord" (2 Chron. 12:1, NIV). As long as Rehoboam was struggling and needed help solving his problems he was willing to trust God for help and solutions. However, after he became comfortable in his position and knew how to solve the problems and run the kingdom, he abandoned his trust in God.

This is a terrible thing for a leader to do, because notice what happened to the followers. Rehoboam not only abandoned his trust and reliance on God, but all of his followers did the same. Leaders have a great influence on their followers and subordinates. We must be very careful that we provide the proper godly example for them to follow. If you trust God and openly give Him the praise and credit, then the followers will tend to do the same. On the other hand, if you take all the credit and forsake God, don't expect anything different from those following you.

Look at the warning God gives the Children of Israel in Deuteronomy 6:10-12: "When the Lord your God brings you into the land He swore to your fathers . . . a land with large, flourishing cities you did not build, houses filled with all kinds of good things you did not provide, wells you did not dig, and vineyards and olive groves you did not plant—then when you eat and are satisfied, be careful that you do not forget the Lord, who brought you out of Egypt, out of the land of slavery" (NIV).

God is warning His people not to stop trusting Him when they have finally succeeded in taking the land He had promised. As long as we are in the midst of the struggle to achieve success it is easy to rely on God because we recognize we must have His help. However, as soon as we achieve our goals of success, the temptation is to stop trusting God and begin trusting in our own strength, position, authority, and experience.

It is extremely dangerous for our spiritual growth and development as well as for the growth and success of our management career to stop trusting God and begin relying on ourselves. The Book of 2 Chronicles, chapters 14–16, tells the story of King Asa.

In the early part of Asa's career he faithfully trusted God. He had many serious problems to face and in each instance he relied on God to help him lead and manage his kingdom. However, as time went by, Asa became more and more self-sufficient. He was a very successful king and greatly respected for his ability. Slowly he began to stop trusting God and to rely on himself and others for his success. As a result, he no longer was blessed by God. As he became less successful he started getting bitter toward God.

Notice how 2 Chronicles 16:12 describes the latter part of Asa's management and leadership career. "In the thirty-ninth year of his reign Asa was afflicted with a disease in his feet. Though his disease was severe, even in his illness he did not seek help from the Lord, but only from the physicians" (NIV). What a tragic end to a very great and godly leader's career.

Asa's life story should serve as a constant reminder of the temptation to stop trusting God for our successes. God is not only the one who makes us successful, He is also the one who keeps us successful, and we must never forget that.

3. *To start interpreting God's Word to fit your own interests.* This is one of Satan's favorite methods of destroying the manager's success. Many leaders fall for this trap because they think they are justified in their disobedience to God's Word.

King Saul, the first king of Israel, is a classic example of a great leader yielding to this temptation. The story of Saul's management and leadership career is found in 1 Samuel, chapters 9–31. It begins in triumph and ends in tragedy. The curtain opens on Saul's leadership career in chapter 9, verses 15-16: "Now the day before Saul came, the Lord had revealed this to Samuel: 'About this time tomorrow I will send you a man from the land of Benjamin. Anoint him leader over My people Israel; he will deliver My people from the hand of the Philistines" (NIV).

God had appointed Saul as the king of the nation of Israel. God blessed his efforts, making him successful in everything he did. However, when Saul went to fight the Philistines he found himself in severe difficulty. Saul and his men were greatly outnumbered and Samuel, the priest, had not arrived to offer the sacrifices to

God prior to battle. In the midst of the pressure of the situation Saul bent the rules of God to fit his own needs.

Notice what Saul did. "So he [Saul] said, 'Bring me the burnt offering and the fellowship offerings.' And Saul offered up the burnt offering" (1 Sam. 13:9, NIV). According to God's laws and regulations, only the priest was allowed to offer the sacrifices and offerings. However, in his distress, Saul had bent God's rules to meet his own need.

When Samuel arrived he asked what Saul had done. Saul replied, "When I saw that the men were scattering, and that you did not come at the set time, and that the Philistines were assembling at Micmash, I thought, 'Now the Philistines will come down against me at Gilgal, and I have not sought the Lord's favor.' So I felt compelled to offer the burnt offering" (1 Sam. 13:11-12, NIV).

Saul used the excuse of a bad situation to justify bending God's rules. It is easy for Christians in leadership positions to be similarily tempted. A close look at Saul's life can help us to learn from his mistakes.

Look at how Samuel responded to Saul's statement. " 'You acted foolishly,' Samuel said. 'You have not kept the command the LORD your God gave you; if you had, He would have established your kingdom over Israel for all time. But now your kingdom will not endure; the LORD has sought out a man after His own heart and appointed him leader of His people, because you have not kept the LORD's command" (1 Sam. 13:13-14, NIV).

It is a dangerous thing to start interpreting God's Word to fit your own interests. It eventually cost Saul his position, career, and life as a leader. And like King Asa, Saul turned his back on God. Saul certainly should be a lesson to all managers and leaders. We may try to justify bending God's rules, but we won't escape the results.

4. *To start thinking you are exempt from God's laws.* The further up the organizational ladder we climb, the more power and authority we have. And the more power and authority we have, the easier it is to start thinking we are exempt from God's laws. Some people actually convince themselves that God's laws do not apply to them. They know what is right, but deliberately disobey God's laws and principles and think that somehow they will escape punishment.

When studying the Old Testament you see numerous occasions where the Children of Israel saw themselves as exempt from God's laws. Judges 2:11-12 states, "Then the Israelites did evil in the eyes of the Lord and served the Baals. They forsook the Lord, the God of their fathers, who had brought them out of Egypt. They followed and worshiped various gods of the people around them" (NIV).

How could a nation who saw God do such great things for them forsake Him? It didn't happen all at once. God warned the people about taking credit for their success. But the nation slowly yielded to those temptations. They eventually thought they were exempt from the Lord's laws and started serving other gods.

The same temptations face leaders today. Never forget that God is responsible for your success. Remain humble before Him and thank Him daily for what He does for and through you. No matter how successful you become, always give God the credit and praise.

Remember, "Pride goes before destruction, a haughty spirit before a fall" (Prov. 16:18, NIV). To remain a successful manager, give God credit for your success and faithfully work at applying His principles in your life and work.

THE RESPONSIBILITY THAT ACCOMPANIES SUCCESS

The more successful we are the greater responsibility we have to share with others what God has given us. In 1 Timothy 6:17-18 we are told: "Command those who are rich in this present world not to be arrogant nor to put their hope in wealth, which is so uncertain, but to put their hope in God, who richly provides us with everything for our enjoyment. Command them to do good, to be rich in good deeds, and to be generous and willing to share" (NIV). We are called to meet the needs of others. Therefore, I would ask you, what is your motive for wanting to be successful? Are you seeking success simply to meet your own personal desires, interests, and needs? If so, according to God's Word, you have the wrong motive. In this chapter we have seen that success brings with it a great responsibility to serve the needs of others. And it is only as we serve that we experience the real meaning and benefit of true success.

PERSONAL APPLICATION

1. What was your definition of success before reading this chapter? Has it changed any?
2. What is the difference between the world's view of success and God's view?
3. Read Revelation 3:17-19.
   a. What principles relating to success are being taught in this passage?
   b. Why do so many people focus on material success, but overlook spiritual success?
4. Why do so many people think that success will bring them happiness?
5. What is the source of true happiness?
6. Study Psalm 32:1-2 and Psalm 119:1-2. What do we learn about true happiness from those passages?
   a. What are you doing in your life to cultivate true happiness?
   b. Can you be successful without applying these passages in your life? Why or why not?
7. What temptations have you faced as you have become more successful?
8. Study the section of this chapter entitled, "Temptations that come with success."
   a. Which of these temptations, if any, do you struggle with the most? Why? How should you deal with those temptations?
   b. In your opinion, why do managers and leaders face these temptations?
   c. What is the end result of yielding to these temptations?
9. What kinds of responsibilities do we have as we become more and more successful as managers and leaders? How do you intend to meet those responsibilities?
10. How will you use the principles in this chapter to better develop your management and leadership skills?

3

HOW TO MANAGE IN
THE MIDST OF CHANGE

During this century the world has experienced greater and more rapid change than all previous centuries combined. Every area of life in our modern day societies has been greatly affected by this phenomenon we call change. Change has revolutionized our lives. Experts tell us that even greater, more rapid, and dramatic changes await our world as we enter the twenty-first century.

As much as any other single group, the manager is one of the people most affected by change. And the manager's potential for success depends, in part, on how well he or she manages in the midst of change.

Carl Williams, a good friend and former client who is a divisional vice president of a large manufacturing firm, recently told me many of his managers are having severe difficulty coping with the rapid changes occurring within their industry. He told me, "The technological advancements in the industry are shaking our business to the very core. It's almost like we're trying to maintain business as normal during the midst of a violent earthquake. There isn't one department not being greatly affected by the changes that are occurring."

He pointed out that these technological changes are opening up whole new markets for their business, but at the same time creating many new problems. "Our people are under a lot more stress than they used to be," he said. "And unfortunately, some of our managers are having a very difficult time managing in the midst of these changes."

He explained that change requires managers to take more risks. He continued, "The greater the risks the greater the possibility of mistakes and failures. Many of our managers are discovering that in order to be effective in managing change they must first do a more thorough job of gathering the facts."

As we continued our conversation Carl shook his head, and with a great deal of concern said, "Myron, it's unfortunate, but we have to face the fact that a lot of our managers just aren't going to survive these days unless they are able to effectively cope with and properly manage the continual changes that are occurring within our business."

MANAGING IN THE MIDST OF CHANGING VALUES

One of the first areas we need to look at is the rapidly changing morals and values of our society. While conducting research for this book I recently interviewed numerous executives and read many books on the management of change. Unfortunately, not one person or book dealt with the impact society's rapidly changing morals and values are having on organizations and people's ability to manage effectively.

From our top national leaders right on down through the ranks to the lowest position within the smallest organization, the prevailing attitude seems to be anything is legal as long as you don't get caught. And unfortunately, more evidence continues to surface of top leaders within Christendom falling prey to this same destructive philosophy. And if some of our top leaders are being deceived, God only knows how much of the church has been infected by this disease.

For example, recently while conducting a series of seminars in Canada on "burnout," the pastor of a very successful church came to me and said, "I am very concerned about many of my peers in the ministry." We discussed the various pressures and problems pastors and other Christian leaders are facing today, and then he said, "Today ministers and Christian leaders are experiencing just as many temptations as anyone else in society, and unfortunately, sometimes we don't do any better job withstanding those temptations than the average person on the street."

During our conversation he pointed out that within the past six months eight of his friends in the ministry had gotten divorced, another had been asked to leave the church because of immorality, and one had committed suicide.

If you want to develop your management potential, then you must learn to manage effectively during the midst of change. And the place to begin is to make sure you are properly managing yourself. Focus on the following:

- Don't compromise your personal morals and values.
- Don't try to ignore the decaying morals and values in your community and organization.
- Speak out on the importance of developing and maintaining high morals and values.

Don't compromise your personal morals and values. As I indicated during the first chapter, instead of dwelling on what managers "do," this book focuses more on what you must "be" as a person if you wish to develop your full potential as a manager. One of the things you must *be* is a person with high morals and uncompromising values.

Our society is all too eager and ready to compromise personal morals and values for the sake of getting what it wants. As a manager, you will frequently find yourself in a position of being tempted, and maybe even asked by higher management, to compromise your personal morals, values, and convictions.

I first met Jess Rosenberg on an elk hunting trip in western Colorado. I spent an entire week tromping around in the mountains of West Elk Wilderness with Jess, and about halfway through our hunt Jess began opening up and talking to me about his life.

I found that he had been the head of the accounting department for a large wholesale distributing company on the East Coast. His wife had been raised in a very wealthy family and it was extremely difficult for him to maintain for them the standard of living to which she had been accustomed. He said, "I had a real good job and was making very good money, but it wasn't enough for her expensive taste."

We were walking along a high ridge looking for elk as Jess told me his story. He continued. "I began to realize that it was going to take a lot more money to support her than I could make at my job. She was a beautiful girl, lots of fun, and I really loved her. So I began trying to figure out ways of making extra cash."

Wiping his brow with the back of his arm he said, "I still can't believe what I allowed myself to get involved with." And with that statement he fell quiet.

The following silence made me wonder if he regretted bringing up the subject. For the next hour I forgot all about about hunting elk as I listened to a man slowly and painfully unfold the story of the past ten years of his life.

He had been raised in a Christian home and accepted Jesus Christ as his personal Saviour at a young age. He had met his wife while in college. After graduation they were married and he went to work as an accountant with the wholesale distributing firm on the East Coast. He was a hard worker and advanced very quickly.

Since his wife had not been exposed to Christianity, and he was usually tired on the weekends, he never insisted that they go to church; however, he tried to live a good life and maintained a high moral code of ethics. But as he began to get further in debt by providing his young bride with the lifestyle she was accustomed to living, he began to realize he could never supply her financial needs on his salary alone.

One day he was discussing his dilemma with a friend at work who offered to let him in on a deal that would make both of them a lot of money fast. He met his friend at a local bar after work and learned that he was involved in financing a small-time drug dealer.

"I couldn't believe what I was hearing," Jess said with a great deal of pain and regret in his voice. "This guy was simply fronting the money for the drugs and making a fabulous return on his investment in a very short period of time. I knew it was wrong, but you weren't actually involved in selling the drugs, and the money was so good that I agreed to team up with my friend and go after even bigger deals."

Within a very short period of time Jess was making much more in the drug business than on his job. Everything was going great for him until the police made a raid on the drug dealers and they named Jess and his friend as the money people behind them. Instead of being able to provide the kind of lifestyle his wife wanted, Jess wound up in prison and lost both his wife and his job.

As I listened to Jess' story I was reminded of the story Jesus told of the wise and foolish builders: "Therefore everyone who hears these words of Mine and puts them into practice is like a wise man who built his house on the rock. The rain came down, the streams rose, and the winds blew and beat against the house; yet it did not fall, because it had its foundation on the rock. But everyone who hears these words of Mine and does not put them into practice is like a foolish man who has built his house on sand. The rain came down, the streams rose, and the winds blew and beat against that house, and it fell with a great crash" (Matt. 7:24-27, NIV).

Jesus is teaching a very important principle of life. We need to build our lives on the strong, solid, and secure principles found in God's Word. When we do, we will discover that our lives are safe no matter how strong life's trials. To build on any other foundation is a mistake. Because when the storms of life come sweeping down against you, like the house built on sand, you will fall with a great crash. Jess Rosenberg certainly proved in his own life the truth of Jesus' teaching.

To develop your full potential as a manager you first must learn how to manage in the midst of change. You must learn to anchor your life strongly on the unchanging principles of God's Word. Only then will you be able to withstand the forces in society that tempt you to buy into the world's value system.

Don't ignore the decaying morals and values in your community and organization. A nation, society, or organization is never any stronger than the moral fiber of its people. And the morality of the people will never be stronger than that of their leaders. Therefore, as a manager/leader in an organization you have a great responsibility not only to lead the way in setting the moral values and standards for the people, but also by challenging those values that serve to undermine your organization's strength and ability to achieve its goals. Be on the lookout for such secular infections.

Speak out on the importance of developing and maintaining high morals and values. It takes people with strong character to effectively deal with the many forces of change at work within our world.

In order to effectively manage midst the winds of change the manager must first have his own feet planted on something solid. That *something* is his own moral code. It provides the stability by which he and the rest of the organization is able to properly manage the changes that constantly occur within the group. Don't be afraid to speak out for the necessity of values in your organization. To fail to do so may ultimately allow the kinds of changes to occur that will destroy instead of strengthen your organization.

CHANGE IS NECESSARY FOR SURVIVAL AND GROWTH

Change is absolutely essential for any organization to meet the ongoing needs of people within our modern, space-age society. For an organization to grow strong it must *always focus on implementing changes that strengthen, instead of weaken, its position.*

When dealing with change, always answer one question: How will this change strengthen the organization? If you can't show positive evidence for the change, then you should seriously question the change before allowing it to be implemented.

A quick study of corporate and organizational history will quickly educate one to the fact that few man-made organizations have been able to successfully develop and maintain the changes necessary to continue serving and meeting the needs of people year after year and century after century.

A wonderful example is the Hudson's Bay Company, founded on May 2, 1670 in England by Prince Rupert and seventeen fellow investors. It is known as the world's oldest continuous capitalist corporation. It began as a company that concentrated solely on the sale of furs, but as society's needs changed it branched out into such businesses as the sale of ice, real estate, oil, and a modern-day department store chain. It is currently bringing in approximately $5 billion in sales annually.

There is only one reason the Hudson's Bay Company is still in existence—it was able to change to meet the demands of the people it served. History clearly teaches that organizations and businesses unable to make the adjustments necessary to meet the constantly changing needs of people do not survive long.

HINDRANCES TO MANAGING CHANGE

There are many hindrances in the way of effectively managing change. In some instances these hindrances are so severe that it becomes virtually impossible to bring about change. And as we have already seen, the inability to change can, and probably will, eventually bring death to the organization.

The most common hindrances to managing change are listed below:

- Being contented with tradition.
- The purpose of the change is not clearly understood.
- There appears to be too much risk involved.
- The people affected by the change are not properly involved in planning and implementing the change.
- It is believed the change will be too costly.

Being contented with tradition. Yesterday's innovations become today's traditions that block the changes that will be needed tomorrow. Contentment with tradition is one of the major hindrances to the development of desperately needed innovations.

We all tend to be creatures of habit. Once we find a method that works we tend to stick with it. We know our way works. Why run the risk of trying something new that might not work as well as the method we have perfected? Yes, practice does make perfect. However, "perfect" is not always best, especially when there is a better way.

The recent explosion of technology should teach us that today's "best way" will be obsolete tomorrow. Unless we are continually examining our traditions and "sacred cows," and looking for better ways and methods, we will soon discover that our entire organization has faded into obsolescence. And when that occurs, we will no longer be meeting the rapidly changing needs of people and society.

Gary Jenkins owns an accounting business that he bought from his uncle. He once told me the company was in shambles when he took it over. He said, "Years ago when I went to work for my uncle he bragged about the fact that we still used manual typewriters in the offices while every other business had converted to electric typewriters. And when other accounting firms started using computers he bragged about the fact that we still did everything by hand."

Gary said that when he finally convinced his uncle to sell him the business there was almost nothing left to buy. "Many years ago my uncle's accounting firm had the reputation of being the biggest and best in the state. However, he was so opposed to change that by the time I finally was able to buy the firm it consisted of only a few accounts of some faithful clients.

It took Gary several years to rebuild the reputation of the firm and convince some of the larger accounts that he could meet their needs for fast and on-time printouts of their business transactions. He installed computers and hired computer programmers capable of designing programs to meet the individual needs of each of his clients. And as new and improved software became available, he continually upgraded in an effort to provide the best possible service to his customers. He hired aggressive accountants trained in the use of the latest computer technology and brought in a sales staff to market his services to the business community. Today, Gary's accounting firm is once again recognized as one of the best in the state. However, unlike his uncle, Gary is constantly looking for innovations that will allow him to continue to serve the rapidly changing needs of his clients.

Gary's example is a model to emulate. Instead of focusing on the traditions that brought you your success, start searching for the innovations that will continue making you successful in the future.

The purpose of the change is not clearly understood. The lack of information regarding the change frequently causes needless rumors that can be detrimental to the implementation of the change. When implementing change, make sure you properly explain both the need and purpose of all the changes and actions.

When the J.C. Penney Company announced its plans to move its corporate headquarters from New York City to Plano, Texas, many of the employees were upset. Rumors began filtering through the organization concerning the possibility of layoffs and loss of job. The company ultimately had to expand its counseling staff from one person to twelve to handle the emotionally upset employees.

A few years ago Phillips Petroleum Company laid off 6,800 employees, and these changes within the corporation produced far-reaching effects, both within the firm as well as in Bartlesville, Oklahoma, headquarters for the corporate offices. Shortly following that major change a local counseling center for abused families reported that requests for assistance increased 69 percent and women attending sessions for battered wives increased 41 percent.

I share these grim statistics with you to illustrate how damaging change can be on individuals within an organization, especially if those changes aren't properly handled. It is extremely important for potentially negative changes to be handled properly. The purpose of the change must be clearly explained to everyone involved and every effort made to make such negative changes as painless as possible.

I used to be a corporate director of personnel for an electronic manufacturing company. One of my most distasteful jobs involved conducting "exit interviews" with managers and executives who were being terminated. On several occasions, I found myself sitting across the desk from a manager who came to work that morning thinking he was doing a satisfactory job, only to learn before the first morning coffee break that he was fired. Handling such negative change experiences made me keenly aware of the need for proper communication in the organization.

There appears to be too much risk involved. The greater the perceived risk, the more difficult it is to effectively implement and manage change. When dealing with change, always properly explain the amount of risk involved. Make sure you, as the manager, have properly evaluated the risks and then communicate those risks to all concerned.

The more people understand the risk involved in making a change, the more they will be able to effectively implement and maintain the change. However, the reverse is also true. The less people understand the risks involved in a change, the more they will resist implementing and maintaining it.

The people affected by the change are not properly involved in planning and implementing the change. If you want change to be implemented and carried out smoothly, make sure that the people affected by the change are properly involved in both its planning and implementation.

For example, as the early church grew in Jerusalem some of the disciples began complaining that many of the widows weren't being properly cared for. Instead of making the decisions and implementing the plans and changes for the people, the leaders had those directly involved in the situation develop the plan for solving the problem (Acts 6:1-5). The plans were made easily because those affected were directly involved in developing and carrying it out. The more you can involve people affected by the plan the more smoothly the changes will be accepted and carried out.

It is believed the change will be too costly. The manager's ability to implement and manage change is greatly hindered when people believe the change will be too costly. Therefore, it is important to show how feasible the plan is to those involved in approving and carrying out the changes. Communication of the feasibility of the changes is absolutely essential to the smooth acceptance, implementation, and application of the changes.

DEVELOPING THE RIGHT ATTITUDE TOWARD CHANGE

The manager's attitude plays an important role in determining the success or failure of the changes being implemented. If the manager sees the changes as positive, then those under him will be more apt to also view the changes as positive. On the other hand, if the manager is negative, his subordinates will tend to consider the changes as negative.

When dealing with changes always focus on the following:
- Recognize and promote the positive aspects of the change.
- Realize that change is the key to organizational renewal.
- Change is the key to personal growth and development.

Recognize and promote the positive aspects of the change. We can always find something negative, even in the best of changes. And during change there is a tendency to concentrate on what is wrong instead of what is right.

During change there is an increase of anxiety, frustration, and fear because the new and unknown is replacing the old, established, and familiar practices. As a result, people tend to be under more stress and are more susceptible to negative thoughts, feelings, and actions.

For example, notice what Proverbs 15:15 tells us in The Living Bible: "When a man is gloomy, everything seems to go wrong; when he is cheerful, everything seems right!" This verse points out the impact our attitude has on results. Positive attitudes tend to help create positive results, and negative attitudes promote negative results. Guard your attitude during the midst of change. Focus on the positive points of the change instead of the negative aspects. You will be much more effective in managing change.

Recognize that change is the key to organizational renewal. Without change your organization will wither and die. Change is the ingredient that continues to renew organizations. It allows an organization to continually meet the needs of people. In fact, organizational change should always be in response to the changing needs of people and society.

As you manage in the midst of change, realize that the more effectively you manage change, the more opportunities your organization will have to continue serving the changing needs of people.

Change is the key to personal growth and development. Change is not only the key to organizational survival; it is also the key to personal growth and development. The absence of change always produces an absence of creativity. Without change there is a lack of opportunity for creative expression. People must have a climate that promotes change to be creative. And creativity gives birth to future change.

For years I have been telling managers during seminars, "When we prevent change because of our fears—our worse fears will always come true!" That statement is truer today because of the rapidly changing needs of people and society.

When you prevent change, you destroy people's ability to be creative. When you stop creativity, you destroy the possibility of future change. An organization that stops changing soon dies because it loses its ability to meet the changing needs of the people it once served. Fears wind up becoming self-fulfilling prophecies.

Take advantage of opportunities to create a climate within your organization that encourages change, not just for change's sake, but for the sake of the changing needs of people. As you do, you will discover that change plays a crucial role in the development of your management potential.

PERSONAL APPLICATION

1. Do you feel your organization promotes or discourages change?
2. Do you as a manager/leader promote or discourage change?

3. What changes are needed within your organization to more effectively meet the needs of people for which it was designed to serve?
4. What changes are needed within the organization to better serve the needs of employees?
5. As a leader what changes do you need to make to better serve the organization and its employees?
6. Read Matthew 7:24-27.
   a. What changes do you need to make in your moral values for them to be more in line with God's Word?
   b. Do you feel your organization needs to improve in the area of values and ethics? If so, in what ways?
7. What will you do to encourage the needed changes within and outside the organization?
8. How will you use the principles in this chapter to better develop your management and leadership skills?

4

COMMIT TO SERVICE
AS A LIFESTYLE

What are the most important aspects of any business or organization? During management seminars I usually ask that question and I'm always amazed at the response. People tend to list such things as: strong financial backing, a competent management team, highly trained and skilled people, a good sales force, and a good product. Some even mention the importance of operating on biblical principles. However, very few people list *service* among the important aspects of any business or organization.

This neglect of service is indicative of a society that is becoming more self-centered. We have become a society committed to being served instead of serving. Our focus is on getting instead of giving.

For most groups service has been relegated to nothing more than a "customer complaint department." However, a customer complaint department does not mean service to customers; on the contrary, it is a sign that service has been greatly lacking. Service must be the "lifestyle" of the entire organization, not something done in a department designed for that purpose.

WHAT IS SERVICE?

The individual seeking to develop his or her full potential as a manager should commit to service as a *lifestyle*. As figure 1 on page 52 illustrates, the manager should recognize that service is to become the objective in all dealings.

As I indicated previously, Matthew 20:25-28 is one of the key passages for the individual desiring to adopt biblical principles of management. Let's look at the passage again in light of the importance of service as a lifestyle. "Jesus called them together and said, 'You know that the rulers of the Gentiles lord it over them, and their high officials exercise authority over them. Not so with you. Instead, whoever wants to become great among you must be your servant, and whoever wants to be first must be your slave—just as the Son of man did not come to be served, but to serve, and give His life as a ransom for many" (Matt. 20:25-28, NIV).

Jesus commands us to serve the needs of others. To provide service to others means we must put others first. A commitment to service as a lifestyle involves a commitment to serving others as a lifestyle. We take on the lifestyle of a servant. An organization or business that makes a commitment to service is simply committing to serving the needs of others.

To provide services involves first becoming a servant. That is why service is so greatly lacking in most businesses and organization in this country today. People aren't willing to assume the role of a servant. We all want to be served, but very few of us are willing to serve.

Figure 1 illustrates service as a lifestyle. The manager's role is to serve the needs of his subordinates, supervisors, peers, and customers. The sole responsibility is to be of service to others.

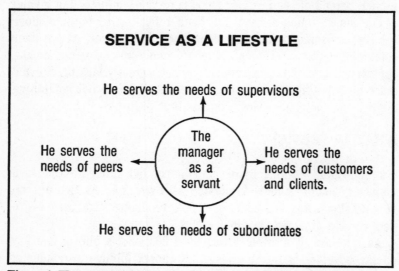

SERVICE AS A LIFESTYLE

He serves the needs of supervisors

He serves the needs of peers ← The manager as a servant → He serves the needs of customers and clients.

He serves the needs of subordinates

Figure 1: The manager who adopts service as a lifestyle commits to serving the needs of those he relates to on a professional basis.

However, most managers tend to use the power of their position to serve themselves instead of others. You will never be able to adopt service as a lifestyle as long as you use the power of your position to serve personal interests.

SERVICE BEGINS WITH MANAGEMENT

Most organizations want their employees to serve the needs of their customers and clients. However, management can't expect employees to be enthusiastic about serving the customer unless the managers are first enthusiastic about serving the needs of their employees. The manager must become the "service role model" for the employee to follow. It is only as the management team enthusiastically serves the employee that the employee enthusiastically serves the client.

The Burdick Companies of Syracuse, New York has a long tradition of being committed to service as a lifestyle. Lou Bregou, one of the company's executives, recently told me, "We learned the hard way that if we wanted employees committed to serving the customer, we first had to develop a management team committed to serving the employees. We discovered that the more excited our managers get about serving the employees the more excited the employee gets about serving the customer."

Several months ago I had an opportunity to spend two days interviewing employees of The Burdick Companies. I talked to a wide cross section of people, both in supervisory and nonsupervisory positions. I was amazed at the employees' commitment to service.

During my conversations a young employee said, "I applied for a job here because one of my friends has worked here a long time and was always telling me what a great company this is. She was right. The managers here are truly concerned about you as an employee and work at meeting our needs."

Another employee told me, "There is an atmosphere of service here. You can feel it when you walk into one of our stores. I still feel it every day when I come to work, and I've worked here for almost five years." When I asked him to explain why everyone was so committed to service he responded, "It's our managers. This is the first place I've worked where the managers actually practice what they preach. But they don't just preach it at us, they practice it on us. They really try to serve us and our needs the way they expect us to serve the needs of the customer."

When I explained to Roger Burdick, one of the owners, how impressed I was with the employees' commitment to service as a company lifestyle he smiled and replied, "Maintaining service as a corporate lifestyle is a full-time job. It's one of our top priorities and it has paid off in many ways other than just increased profits."

Roger explained that as the managers focused on service, the end result was a more motivated and productive work force, making everyone's job more enjoyable and rewarding. Then he said, "Making a decision to make service one of our top priorities is probably one of the best moves we ever made. It's been an important factor in our success."

If you are interested in developing your managerial potential, making a commitment to service as a lifestyle will be one of the most important decisions you will make. Make service a priority in your department, division, or organization. Communicate that priority to your people; model it before them. Serve their needs first. Let them see you serving the needs of your superiors, your peers, and your customers and clients. Adopt service as a lifestyle; then you will have a right to expect those under you to make a commitment to service as well.

Jesus Christ is our perfect role model when it comes to service. He spent His life here on earth meeting the needs of others. Jesus didn't just tell His disciples to serve the needs of others, but He told them to follow His example. He didn't come to be served, but to serve to the point of giving His very life for us. Commit to service as a lifestyle not because this management consultant says you should, but because Jesus Christ requires it of all who would follow Him.

WHY SERVICE IS BEING NEGLECTED

During a conversation with Roger Burdick and Lou Bregou of The Burdick Companies, I asked them why service was being neglected in this country. "The word is menial," Roger said. "No one wants to think of himself as a servant. And you have to become a servant in order to provide service. Unfortunately, we have become more concerned with getting things done than how well we do it."

Lou nodded in agreement and added, "Providing service is contrary to our human nature. Most of us are so self-centered we fail to consider the needs of others. We are only thinking of our own needs. There's another reason service is lacking in this country; we don't have many companies providing good role models of service as an organizational lifestyle."

When they decided to make service a major company-wide priority, they began looking for other companies to emulate, but they discovered a general lack of commitment to service on the part of managers and corporate executives. "We also discovered a lack of education concerning how to provide service," Lou continued. "There are lots of books on how to manage, but very few on how to provide good service."

During my conversation with Roger and Lou that day, they listed five reasons why service is being neglected in this country. Their reasons, with some expanded thinking on my part, follow.

1. *Providing service is considered a menial task; therefore, it is an undesirable job to perform.* People do not understand the purpose of business or organizations. The ultimate goal should be to provide a service. Therefore, service becomes the primary function, duty, and task of every job or position within the business or organization.

The person desiring to reach full potential in management must grasp this very important point. Your primary responsibility should be to provide service. As Roger Burdick so aptly stated, "We must continually train ourselves to see things through the customer's eyes. We have been programmed to see things through the organization's eyes and think in terms of what is best for the business. However, our real aim should be to consider what is best for the customer, for only then is service truly our goal."

Service is not a menial task. In fact, quite the contrary is true. Service is the highest calling and most important activity any employee can perform. The manager's job is to demonstrate service in action, as well as teach and train subordinates how to provide it.

Make service a lifestyle both personally and organizationally. Practice service as a personal lifestyle, and teach your subordinates to do the same. Make service a way of life; as you do, you will be developing your potential as a manager.

2. *There is a lack of good organizational role models available.* During the twentieth century, there has been less and less emphasis placed on the importance of service. As we enter the twenty-first century, it is harder to find companies qualified as role models of a service lifestyle. I travel all over the world working with all types of businesses and organizations (including many Christian groups), but I have never seen a business more committed to a service lifestyle than The Burdick Companies. They are rapidly becoming an excellent role model for other groups interested in seeing a corporate service lifestyle in action.

While I was discussing the need for role models with Roger Burdick, he said, "The managers at the top must become the role models for the rest of the organization. They must make a decision that it can be done and take the initiative or nothing will happen. There is no magic involved. It requires a strong commitment. It doesn't require millions of dollars in investments, simply strong conviction and commitment to the principles and then a demonstration of those principles in action on a daily basis."

Lou was quick to agree. He said, "Those of us at the top must set the example by making just as strong a commitment to managing service as we do to managing projects and budgets. Our people don't believe we're committed to service by what we say; they believe we are committed to service because of what we do. We must be the role model and then they will follow our example."

The Burdick Companies' track record is proof that commitment to service plays a major role in developing one's management potential. If you are willing to make the same commitment to service as the leadership team at Burdick made, and start looking at situations from the customer's or subordinate's perspective, you too can experience the same type of positive results.

3. *It is not being emphasized as a part of the training of leaders and managers.* The problem isn't the availability of training and educational material; the problem is the lack of commitment to a service lifestyle. I urge you to commit to service as a

managerial lifestyle. This is the only answer. Begin viewing service as your primary mission as a manager and leader. Begin working to meet the needs of all those around you. And start requiring your subordinates to focus on the needs of those around them.

As Roger Burdick pointed out, there is nothing magic about adopting service as a lifestyle. It is just plain hard work and a day-to-day commitment to serving the needs of others. Roger told me, "It isn't just a trip; it's a lifelong journey. We must daily keep service before us as our top priority. That is how it eventually becomes a way of life with us—a lifestyle."

4. *The goal has been to maximize profits while minimizing effort.* There is nothing wrong with maximizing profits while minimizing effort as long as it doesn't have a negative impact on service. However, in most instances service is one of the first areas we cut in our effort to make more money. Unfortunately, as soon as we begin cutting service we also run the risk of decreasing profits in the future.

While discussing the issue of profit versus service with Lou and Roger, Lou said, "When considering service we tend to focus on short-term instead of long-term results. In the short run more service may mean less profits. However, over the long term, more service will help generate more business and additional profits."

For the past several years The Burdick Companies have been buying financially troubled car dealerships and turning them into profitable businesses. When I asked Roger what he considered to be the key to their success he said, "It's really quite simple. We begin majoring on service. We work hard at meeting the needs of our employees and also the needs of our customers."

Roger pointed out that in some instances the dealerships had been in financial trouble because previous management had attempted to decrease service to make more money. He explained that cutting service is a sure way to start losing a customer's business. "When we buy a dealership that is in financial trouble, we change very little except the focus on service," Roger said. "And as we make service a major priority we begin building a stronger customer base. And since our customers are satisfied with the service we give them, they tell their friends. Our service produces satisfied customers and satisfied customers bring you more and more business. It's as simple as that."

"That's right," Lou agreed. "We must have value to our customers. If we are of value to our customers, we won't have to worry about existing in the future. Therefore, we must address the issue—are we of value to the customer and how will we improve that value? The customer ultimately runs the whole show, and we must never forget that!"

5. *The increasing attitude of "That's not my job!"* As a management consultant I do a lot of traveling. While conducting a management training program in Juneau, Alaska, two boxes of workbooks I was shipping with my luggage failed to arrive at the baggage carousel in Juneau. I went to the ticket counter of the airline that had brought me from Seattle to Juneau and explained the boxes were missing. The ticket agent told me he didn't handle baggage and that I would have to go to the office that handled missing luggage.

I went there, but the office was closed. I went back to the ticket counter, talked to a different agent, explained my problem with the missing boxes and pointed out that the missing luggage office was closed. She also told me luggage was not her department, she only issued tickets, but she finally gave me a toll free number to call in Seattle.

When I called the number I was told that office did not deal with missing luggage and was given a different number to call. I called that number and was told to check with their luggage department in Juneau. When I explained the office was closed in Juneau, I was given another number to call. I called that number only to get a recorded message informing me that I would have to call back during regular business hours the next day.

Extremely frustrated, I went to my hotel room. The first thing the next morning I called the airport again concerning my boxes. No one knew anything about missing boxes, so I called the last number I had been given the night before. I was told I had the wrong office; they didn't deal with missing luggage. When I asked who did, I was told, "I don't know, but we don't!" Then I was told to check with the ticket counter at the Juneau Airport.

I realized I was facing a hopeless situation. The seminar was to start in less than an hour and someone had lost the workbooks I needed for the participants. Since no one was willing to assume responsibility for helping locate my missing boxes, I had to conduct the seminar without the workbooks.

When I returned to my office in Colorado Springs a few days later, there was a message asking me to call the airline. I called the number and was asked what I wanted done with the two boxes of workbooks that had been in the Juneau airport for the past several days. I discovered that the boxes had arrived on a flight two hours earlier than mine, and one of the attendants had put them behind a desk in the office that handled missing luggage. The boxes had been in Juneau all the time, but no one had been willing to assume the responsibility of helping me locate them.

When we have the attitude, "That's not my job," we are failing to provide the kind of service that meets the needs of the customer. And when the customer's needs are not met, we eventually lose that customer. I will be very reluctant to fly on that airline again!

BIBLICAL PRINCIPLES OF SERVICE

When considering service as a lifestyle, we must ultimately deal with an important question: How do I determine how much service to render? The Bible's two key passages on business ethics also provide principles for answering this question.

Let's look first at Matthew 7:12: "In everything, do to others what you would have them do to you, for this sums up the Law and the Prophets" (NIV). Jesus is discussing the kind of lifestyle we should maintain in relating to others. In all our business dealings—with subordinates, superiors, peers, and customers—we are to treat them in the same way we would want to be treated.

We are to provide the same amount of service we would expect to receive. Our own standard of expectations is the answer to the amount and type of service we should provide to others. The principle is extremely easy to understand; however, it is the application that is difficult.

The second passage providing us with biblical principles of service is found in Matthew 5:40-41: "And if someone wants to sue you and take your tunic, let him have your cloak as well. If someone forces you to go one mile, go with him two miles" (NIV). This passage deals with how we respond to legal requirements that are placed on us. If we are sued in a court of law, and we legally owe someone our tunic, we should give our cloak as well.

What is the principle being taught here as it relates to service? It seems to me Jesus is teaching us that we are to do more than what is required of us by law. Our service should go beyond the minimum requirements covered by the warranty.

With issues of service, we should be willing to do more than we are legally required to fulfill a contract or warranty. We should cheerfully go beyond the minimum requirements of what the law requires when providing service to people.

The next verse reinforces that principle. If we are forced to go one mile, we should go two. In other words, do more than is required of you. The secular world will usually do what the law requires, or what they are being forced to do. However, Jesus is teaching us that we are not to serve the way the secular world serves. The service we render should go beyond what is required or expected.

SERVICE VS. PROFIT

Service is the very core of what management is all about. Service should be the foundation upon which all businesses and organizations are built. It should be the major motivating factor behind everything that happens. Service should be the focal point of our management and corporate lifestyles. A company's value is in direct proportion to the amount of service it provides.

Lasting value is not measured in terms of profit, but in terms of service rendered. You may cut costs, reduce service, and show an increase in profit for a given year. But eventually you will drive customers away because of this lack of service. And as your customers go, so goes your profits. Profits do not exist without customers, and customers don't exist without good service.

We need to remind ourselves that it is ultimately "service" that generates profits, because service brings in the customers. If more and better service brings in more customers and in turn creates the possibility of more profits, then service ultimately is the most important factor in determining the lasting value of an organization or business. The real *bottom line* is not how much profit are we making, but how much service are we providing?

YOU HAVE A CHOICE TO MAKE

As a leader and manager you have a choice to make. You must decide: *"Will I pattern my management lifestyle after the secular world's philosophy, or will I pattern it after the teachings of Jesus Christ?"* This is the most important choice you will make in your career.

You may not be ready to make a decision to choose between the two. You need to realize that a failure to choose is, in fact, a choice to maintain a management lifestyle patterned after the world's philosophy.

The world says, "Serve self." Jesus said, "Serve others." As a manager and leader, you will develop a lifestyle that does one or the other. Which will it be? We all choose. We either serve self or serve others in every life situation. Follow the example of Jesus Christ and His teachings and philosophy. Commit to service as your management and personal lifestyle.

PERSONAL APPLICATION

1. In what ways has service been deteriorating in this country?
2. In what ways has service been getting better?
3. What are the things that tend to hinder businesses and organizations from providing better service?
4. Why is it important for managers to adopt service as a lifestyle? Are you prepared to do so? If not, why not?
5. How would you rate the level of service in your business or organization? How can it be improved?
6. Read Matthew 7:12, Matthew 5:39-42, and Philippians 2:3-4.
   a. Why is it difficult to apply these passages in your businesses and organizations?
   b. How can you more effectively apply them on a day-to-day basis?
   c. Develop a plan to begin incorporating service into your management and organizational lifestyle.

7. What will you do to begin training others within your business or organization in adopting a lifestyle of service?

5

THE ROLE RENEWAL
PLAYS IN SUCCESS

I live in the Colorado Rockies. One of my favorite ways to spend a weekend is exploring the multitude of four-wheel drive roads that have been carved into the mountainsides and along the valley floors. We call them "jeep roads."

One weekend I threw some camping gear into the back of my four-wheel drive pickup and headed west out of Woodland Park, where I live, toward the Continental Divide and some jeep roads I had wanted to explore for a long time.

After driving for a couple of hours I turned off the main highway and began slowly making my way up a long valley that steadily rose higher and higher into the heart of the snowcapped Rocky Mountains. The further I drove the rougher and steeper the narrow jeep road became. I eventually had to stop and park my truck because erosion had made the road impassable.

I took my binoculars out of my backpack and, climbing a steep hill, began surveying the vast panorama that stretched out for miles on all sides. I soon spotted several old, unpainted, dilapidated log buildings off in the distance and realized I was looking at a ghost town nestled at the base of the valley.

Sitting there I began wondering who had lived there, how the town had started, what had brought people to this rugged country, and what had caused the town to die.

Staring at the bleached, skeletal remains of what had once been a booming town, I was looking at all that remained of the desires, dreams, hopes, and hard work of now gone and probably forgotten people. I kept asking myself, Why did they come here? What did they do here? Why did they leave? And where did they go?

I decided to camp for the night. That evening my mind drifted back across the rugged miles to my own town of Woodland Park perched 8,500 feet above sea level in the mountains a few miles west of Colorado Springs. I began comparing the difference between my community, bustling with activity and growth, and this dead ghost town, and I wondered what had caused one to be so alive and the other so dead.

I thought of the old shack on a corner lot in Woodland Park that had recently been torn down and replaced with a new McDonalds and of the plans for a new shopping center to be built across the street in what is now a vacant field. I realized the difference between my town and this one was that renewal was continually taking place in my town, but it had long since stopped occurring in this empty ghost town.

WHAT IS RENEWAL?

Renewal is the process of making something like new again. Organizational renewal is the process of regrouping and getting back on the right course, creating new life, energy, direction, and purpose.

Renewal involves creating a process of continual innovation designed to allow an organization and its people to make the changes necessary to continually meet the rapidly changing demands of its customers.

Renewal is an ongoing, never-ending process. Like service, it must become an intricate part of the individual and organizational lifestyle. Renewal is a way of life that enables people, businesses, and organizations to shed and avoid the excess baggage that hinders change and flexibility. Renewal breaks down the rigid structures and cumbersome systems of organizational bureaucracy that stifle creativity, innovation, and change.

WHY RENEWAL IS NECESSARY

There are numerous reasons why renewal is necessary. Some of the more important ones are listed below.

- It creates the flexibility for effectively responding to rapid change.

- It helps a business or organization remain or become competitive in the marketplace.
- It enhances the potential for growth.
- It injects new life and energy into the organization.

It creates the flexibility for effectively responding to rapid change. While some individuals, businesses, and organizations are busy bringing about those changes, others are being left far behind. Because society is in such a state of flux, managers must be committed to renewal in their management lifestyle. A commitment to renewal is, in part, a commitment to organizational flexibility. And flexibility is absolutely essential for promoting or keeping pace with change.

A commitment to renewal is a commitment to change because renewal always brings about change. However, change by itself does not constitute renewal. An organization may make several changes without developing renewal as a lifestyle. For example, an organization may be forced to make changes without altering its resistance to change. But the organization adopting renewal as a lifestyle will always welcome change and work toward change as a means of more effectively meeting the changing needs within society.

Back in the mid-1970s, Ryder Systems, a corporation known for its trucking business, was forced to sell five of its businesses just to survive. The company had to make changes against its will. However, today Ryder Systems is eagerly and willingly making changes as a result of its commitment to renewal.

The deregulation of the trucking industry in 1980 forced Ryder Systems to begin rethinking its priorities and refocus its emphasis. Ryder has steadily been shifting its emphasis from trucking to a broader goal of serving the transportation industry as a whole. They have been investing hundreds of millions of dollars in the aviation business and within the past few years have purchased close to fifty smaller businesses as the company continues the process of renewal, and redefines, refocuses, and redirects its energies.

In the past Ryder made changes because it was forced to. However, today the company makes changes because it plans to. A commitment to renewal has led to a commitment to flexibility.

And flexibility has made it easier to make the changes they felt were necessary.

Today, more and more businesses are sensing the need for change. However, many of those organizations have a history of inflexibility and resistance to change. Such groups desperately need to make a commitment to renewal. They need to change their attitude from one that says, "We've always done it this way," to one that emphasizes, "Let's find a better way." However, to find a better way, one must first be willing to become flexible.

It helps a business or organization remain or become competitive in the marketplace. A trip to any K-Mart store will quickly show the observant shopper that competition for the buyer's dollar has reached international proportions. During this century competition has switched from the local arena to the global one. We now purchase our consumer goods from places in the world many of us would have difficulty finding on a map.

As a result, it is becoming more difficult to remain competitive in the marketplace. However, survival depends on the ability to become and remain competitive. Ability to compete determines the ability to survive.

At one point in history the ghost town I visited was alive with activity. Businesses and organizations were successfully competing in the marketplace. Eventually something caused those groups to fail in the marketplace. When the marketplace died, the town died with it.

That is why renewal is becoming critical in modern society. Renewal not only helps an organization become flexible, it encourages the type of creative environment that leads to positive changes that make a competitive edge.

It enhances the potential for growth. There is no longer such a thing as *the status quo* when it comes to organizational growth and development. An organization is either in the process of growing or dying, it never "just stays the same."

As society evolves at an ever-increasing pace, it is necessary for companies to do the same. To avoid obsolescence, both the organization and its people must learn to grow and change with our growing and changing society.

Growth does not necessarily mean an increase in size. An organization can increase in size without the kind of growth that occurs in the renewal process. Growth from the perspective of renewal involves the ability to respond quickly and correctly to the changing needs within society. From the vantage point of renewal, growth means developing your organization until it is on the cutting edge of change.

It injects new life and energy into the organization. Renewal is the new life and energy that creates positive growth and enables an organization to position itself on the cutting edge.

An organization's new life and energy comes from the new ideas that are generated and used. The processes we call "organizational renewal" unlock the unlimited creative potential in the fertile soil we call the human mind, and enables the organization to reap a bumper crop of valuable and innovative ideas. This becomes the cornerstone for building a strong, healthy, and productive organization for the future.

PEOPLE: THE FOCAL POINT OF RENEWAL

Organizational change does not occur by itself; it is brought about by people. For an organization to change, people need to change. People are the focal point of all organizational renewal efforts.

The manager/leader must realize that organizational renewal comes about only as a result of people being committed to personal renewal. For example, during the time of the Jewish exile the people remaining in Jerusalem were very discouraged. People coming from Judah told Nehemiah, "Those who survived the exile and are back in the province are in great trouble and disgrace. The wall of Jerusalem is broken down, and its gates have been burned with fire" (Neh. 1:3, NIV).

Picture that scene. The people living in Jerusalem were living in the midst of ruin and rubble of a destroyed city. They were an easy target for their enemies and greatly discouraged. However, they were doing nothing to improve their situation. And the situation within the city did not change until the people's attitude changed.

In the second chapter of Nehemiah we see him going to Jerusalem to rebuild the city and its wall. However, that was not his first job. He first helped the people renew their willingness to solve the

67

problem. And once that was accomplished, the people said, "Let us rebuild the wall" (Neh. 2:18, NIV), and fifty-two days later they had accomplished the task.

It took only fifty-two days to solve the problems created by the city's destroyed wall. However, the bad situation within the city did not change until the people first changed. They had to renew their faith in themselves and once again believe they could solve their own problems before anything positive happened to solve the city's problem.

The Book of Nehemiah teaches some very important principles concerning renewal, and one of them is that the manager/leader must first help the people experience personal renewal before there can be organizational renewal. The successful manager will realize that renewal begins with people and is accomplished through people.

Renewal involves a transformation of the mind. In Romans 12:2 Paul said, "Do not conform any longer to the pattern of this world, but be transformed by the renewing of your mind" (NIV). The principle being taught here applies to the process of renewal. Transformation begins with the mind. Outward change occurs as a result of inward change. There must be a transformation of thinking patterns for renewal to occur.

To begin solving problems, the manager must first change his attitude toward his employees. Organizational problems usually mean people problems. When a manager experiences problems within his organization or department, he usually tends to blame people for the problem.

Renewal can never begin as long as the manager blames people for the problems. The manager's thinking pattern must change. People should be viewed not as the source of the problem, but as the source of the solutions. The manager's attitude and actions must change. Instead of complaining about the employees and criticizing them, the manager encourages, helps, and motivates them to solve the problems. He taps the unlimited creativity of the human mind. There is a solution to every problem, and the solution will be found by unlocking the creative and innovative ideas of his or her people. This is one of the first important steps in accomplishing organizational renewal.

CREATING AN ENVIRONMENT FOR RENEWAL

Renewal isn't a "system" of management, but rather an environment that management creates. Renewal must begin with management. Unless the manager is committed to renewal on a personal level as well as an organizational level it will not occur. The manager must not only recognize the need for organizational renewal, but emphasize its importance to the employees and then become a role model of renewal in action.

In order to achieve organizational renewal the manager must create the following renewal environment:

- Emphasize the need of innovation and employee creativity.
- Use the planning process to create flexibility.
- Emphasize the need for employees to begin thinking in terms of "opportunity" and "possibility."
- Focus on sharing decision-making power with subordinates.
- Reward innovation.

Emphasize the need of innovation and employee creativity.
The manager must not see only the need for innovation and employee creativity; he or she must begin actively emphasizing that need. Remember, we are discussing making renewal a part of your management lifestyle. Innovation and employee creativity must be emphasized on an ongoing basis, not once a year as an afterthought at the Christmas party or company picnic.

Renewal is built around innovation and creativity. The absence of innovation within an organization breeds stagnation. Stagnation eventually leads to termination. Organizations tend to gravitate toward stagnation instead of innovation. Innovation involves change, and individuals and organizations alike tend to resist change, choosing rather to become creatures of habit. Creating an innovative environment takes a lot of consistent, hard work from the manager. The manager must continually promote and encourage innovation until it becomes a positive habit and the normal way of thinking among employees.

There is only one source of innovative and creative ideas—people. It is the innovative and creative ideas of people that allow an organization to continually renew itself. Therefore, people must be recognized for what they are—an organization's most valuable and important resource. We must never forget that people, not organizations, produce and maintain renewal.

To draw out and promote the innovative and creative ideas of employees, on a regular basis (at least annually) pose the following questions to your people:

● What should we start?
● What should we stop?
● What should we keep?
● What should we change?

These four issues: start, stop, keep, and change should be discussed in light of the six questions: what, who, where, when, why, and how, as illustrated in figure 2 below.

Bringing about renewal through innovation involves dealing with four issues: start, stop, keep, and change. For each issue we ask ourselves the six basic questions: what, who, where, when, why, and how. For example, when dealing with the issue of "start" we would ask ourselves:

● What should we start?
● Who should be involved?
● Where will this happen?
● When will this happen?

BRINGING ABOUT RENEWAL THROUGH INNOVATION						
Issues	questions					
	what	who	where	when	why	how
start						
stop						
keep						
change						

Figure 2: Illustrates the kinds of issues and questions involved in bringing about renewal through innovation.

- Why should this happen?
- How will this happen?

The nature of some issues may make it advantageous to bring in an outside facilitator to assist with the meeting. However, in most cases the organization will find it doesn't need assistance in conducting such sessions. It should be noted that figure 2 can be used for both personal and organizational renewal.

Use the planning process to create flexibility. In most organizations traditional approaches to planning tend to create inflexibility instead of flexibility. As figure 3 illustrates, most planning is designed to help one get from point A to point B in the easiest and shortest way possible. However, the best and most effective route may not always be a straight line.

Traditional, "straight line" planning tends to put blinders on people, making them unaware of better opportunities. In traditional planning we tend to set our sights on a very specific and measurable goal and forge ahead neglecting all other possibilities. Such approaches to planning tend to create rigid mind-sets, very structured operations, and inflexible people, all characteristics extremely detrimental to achieving renewal.

The plan should be the method by which we accomplish a goal. However, in many traditional planning systems (such as Management By Objectives) the plan frequently becomes the goal, losing sight of the original objective. Thus, we must continually remind ourselves that planning is not the "end," it is only the means to the end. Unfortunately, most traditional planning systems, with

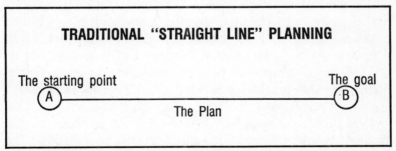

Figure 3: This illustrates how the traditional, straight-line approach to planning tends to seek the shortest and quickest route from the starting point to the goal.

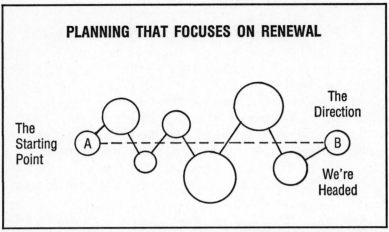

PLANNING THAT FOCUSES ON RENEWAL

The
Starting
Point

A

The
Direction

B

We're
Headed

Figure 4: Planning that focuses on renewal is designed with enough flexibility to enable the organization to examine every opportunity in moving toward its goal.

their emphasis on structure and timetables, do more to hinder renewal than help its development.

Figure 4 above illustrates the model of planning designed to bring about renewal. A represents the starting point, but B represents the direction we're heading instead of the goal. Renewal-focused planning deals more with determining a specific direction, rather than with very specific goals and steps.

However, this does not mean attention is not given to detail with goals, and objectives ignored. The company still sets measurable objectives and identifies the steps involved in accomplishing its plan. But these goals, objectives, and steps are not set in concrete. On the contrary, they serve as guidelines and may be altered quickly as more and better opportunities become available. That is why the straight line between A and B is shown as a dotted instead of a solid line.

Even though the steps have been determined, the plan remains flexible. Positive changes are still welcomed at any time. The organization is still open to new directions. The plan is not considered sacred.

Notice in figure 4 the solid line connecting a series of circles along the path between A and B. These circles represent the numerous possibilities that are systematically explored as the organization continues to pursue the directions of its plan. The line is shown as a solid line because exploring such opportunities is a deliberate part of the ongoing planning process, even though the direction has already been determined.

This approach creates a plan with all the flexibility needed for responding to changing needs, or new and better opportunities. A renewal approach to planning creates a balance between the time, energy, and effort spent determining the steps to accomplish a specific goal and exploring new and better opportunities. Each is considered equally necessary and important, and there is an equally strong commitment to both.

Emphasize the need for employees to begin thinking in terms of "opportunity" and "possibility." Opportunity is all around us. However, only those looking for opportunity see it when it comes. The manager/leader must continually encourage his or her employees to look for new opportunities and better ways of doing things.

We must look for opportunity and possibility in everything we do. One person's obstacle can become an opportunity to learn, solve problems, or reach higher levels of productivity for another person. The renewing individual or organization is constantly thinking in terms of better opportunities and greater possibilities. But more than thinking, they actively pursue and act on them.

Unfortunately, for those bound in the grips of tradition, thinking in terms of opportunities and possibilities can be threatening. Thus, it may take a major crisis before people are even willing to consider the subject. Ironically, in most cases the crisis is the result of failure to consider better opportunities and greater possibilities.

Contemporary examples are plentiful. Ford Motor Company had to experience a serious crisis before it was willing to make the changes that produced quality cars like the Ford Taurus and Mercury Sable. Several years ago it took the threat of bankruptcy before the management team at Chrysler was willing to adopt the attitudes that put the company on the road to renewal. Today, Chrysler Corporation emphasizes a renewal attitude and the result is better service to the customer.

Organizations actively looking for better opportunities and greater possibilities will develop and sustain a renewal lifestyle. Renewal will help insure that you and your organization will not only be around to welcome the twenty-first century, but that you will be able to make a major contribution in molding and shaping its destiny.

Focus on sharing decision-making power with subordinates. Organizational renewal is achieved through greater employee participation in the decision-making processes. For example, it was no accident that the Ford Taurus won *Motor Trend's* 1986 Car of the Year award. Taurus was the result of more than 1,400 ideas generated directly by employees who would be working on the car. The management team at Ford Motor Company has made a new commitment to employee involvement and is actively working at giving employees more decision-making power. The results have been obvious; according to independent research, the quality of Ford cars and trucks has increased, on average, more than 50 percent since 1980.

During the past few years a multitude of companies have proven that greater employee involvement in decision-making does not lead to a loss of control, but on the contrary, it is the key to helping a business or organization gain greater control over its future.

Reward innovation. The environment for renewal is never complete until we begin rewarding people. Make innovation, possibility thinking, and creative planning your standards of performance and reward those who meet them. Build in accountability for renewal and then reward your people for accomplishing it.

Give verbal recognition, promotions and increased responsibility, and financial reward to those employees who make renewal happen. Promote them as the role models. And then be consistent in providing similar recognition to employees who rise to the challenge of becoming directly involved in renewal.

Remember: true organizational renewal requires the involvement of all employees. As the organization begins reaping the benefits of renewal, those involved in creating that benefit should be rewarded accordingly, for only then has the true purpose of renewal gone full cycle.

PERSONAL APPLICATION

1. Are you becoming stagnant as a manager? Why or why not?
2. Do you feel your business or organization is becoming stagnant? Why or why not?
3. What changes do you need to make in your own life to avoid stagnation?
4. What changes need to be made in your department, organization, or business to avoid stagnation?
5. In what areas do you feel a greater need to become flexible as a manager? How will you achieve this?
6. In what areas do you feel your department or organization needs to become more flexible? How will you achieve this?
7. Study the section of the chapter entitled, "Creating an Environment for Renewal" and develop an action plan for applying and implementing each component of the environment.

6

MANAGEMENT TRAITS THAT INFLUENCE POTENTIAL

Recently I attended the wedding of Carl Williams' youngest daughter, and during the reception Carl introduced me to Winford McDonough, his former boss who is now retired. Winford is a very pleasant and jolly gentleman in his early seventies, but he looks and acts many years younger.

With a laugh that lit up the twinkle in his bright, mischievous eyes, he said, "I was the one who hired Carl. But I must admit that shortly after I hired Carl I thought I had made a big mistake. Carl was the most disorganized person I had ever met. You could never find him when you needed him, and he could never figure out where he was supposed to be. He even had a hard time remembering to show up at our regularly scheduled supervisory meetings, and he couldn't even keep his own checkbook balanced!"

Winford patted Carl on the shoulder with as much pride as a father pats his own son and continued. "But just look at Carl today. He's blossomed into one of the best managers in the company. In fact, I predict he will be president of the company someday if he continues in the way he is going."

LEADERS AND MANAGERS ARE "MADE," NOT BORN

Management is a science. And as with any science, management is influenced and governed by the law of cause and effect. The law of cause and effect states that every cause produces a predictable result or "effect." And that certainly is true in most instances within the field of management.

For example, poor organization always produces frustrated and confused employees. Poor planning produces poor results. Specific causes and actions tend to produce predictable results. To improve your management abilities, you must learn to apply the principles and perform the functions that produce effective results within the organization.

Some people have more natural talent and ability than others. However, all of us can learn to cultivate the traits needed to make us effective and productive managers, even though some of us will have to work at it harder than others. In the early days of Carl's career he was a very poor manager. However, today Carl is recognized as one of the most effective managers in his entire corporation. How did that happen? Simply, Carl developed the traits needed to become a highly productive manager/leader.

The Bible provides numerous examples of unskilled people who later became effective leaders. Moses had tried to help his people while they were in Egypt as slaves and failed miserably. As a result of his failure he had to flee the country (Ex. 2:11-15). However, later we see Moses leading the entire nation of Israel out of Egypt to the Promised Land.

David was only a shepherd, but he became one of the greatest kings in Israel's history. And as we have already seen, Nehemiah, the king's cupbearer, became a very effective leader and manager. Peter was just a hot-tempered, commercial fisherman, but he became one of the leaders of the early church.

You can learn, just as managers from Moses to Carl Williams have learned, the skills necessary for becoming an effective manager. In this chapter we will examine the traits that produce both management strengths and weaknesses. You will be given an opportunity to identify the personal traits in your life that are either helping or hindering the development of your managerial potential.

"TRAITS" VS. "STYLE"

During the past few years a multitude of books and articles have been written about management style and the important role it plays in the management of people. However, very little has been written on the subject of management "traits" and their influence on the individual's ability to succeed in management. And I want to suggest to you that one's "management traits" play a much more important role in development of one's management potential than "management style" does.

Leadership style focuses on the use and location of authority. In a "dictatorial management style," the manager retains all the authority and uses it to control others under him. On the other hand, the opposite extreme is the "free-reign management style" in which the manager delegates almost all of the authority to others. Between these two extremes are various other styles in which the manager retains or delegates varying degrees of authority, depending on the style being used.

Management traits deal with "what" and "who" we are as managers. Management traits help influence and determine what we do and don't do, what we accomplish or fail to accomplish, how we act and react in given situations, and how we tend to think and perform on a day-to-day basis.

Traits are learned and cultivated. Even though some people may, by nature, be organized, most management traits can be learned and cultivated. For example, in Titus 1:6-10 Paul describes the type of traits a church leader must have. All of the traits mentioned can be learned and cultivated.

Management traits can be classified as either "strengths" or "weaknesses." All of us develop traits that either help or hinder the development of our management potential. The good manager recognizes those that hinder management and works at eliminating or minimizing them, while at the same time cultivating and developing those that aid and assist.

For example, by nature I have difficulty managing my time. However, I quickly learned that if I wanted to succeed in a management career I had to learn to effectively manage time. I began learning from other managers who had developed the trait of effectively managing time. I worked hard at time management, making it a top priority. I began using good time management tools, such as carrying a pocket calendar, setting priorities for the day and week, working from a daily "do list," and so on. And over a period of time I developed the trait of being organized and managing my time effectively.

Carl Williams was very unorganized when he was hired by Winford McDonough, a trait that certainly would be considered a management weakness. However, Carl worked at overcoming his management weaknesses and began cultivating traits that helped develop his management potential. That is one of the major reasons Carl is a top manager in his company. He worked at overcoming those management traits that would be considered weaknesses, and he developed traits that would become strengths. Carl would be the first to tell you that if he could do it, you can also.

MANAGEMENT TRAITS ANALYSIS SURVEY

In 1976 Management Training Systems, our consulting firm based in Colorado Springs, designed a tool we call Management Traits Analysis Survey. And since that time we have helped thousands of leaders and managers identify their personal traits that were either helping or hindering in their efforts to become better managers.

The survey classifies management traits into four categories. These four categories are called: The Promotional Manager, The Concept Manager, The Operational Manager, and The Negotiating Manager. Each category contains a set of twenty traits that is considered either a weakness or strength as it related to management.

I strongly encourage you to work through the following Management Traits Analysis Survey in order to better understand your own management strengths and weaknesses. Following the survey we will discuss each category separately and explain how to utilize your own management traits to further develop your management potential.

INSTRUCTIONS FOR COMPLETING THE MANAGEMENT TRAITS ANALYSIS SURVEY:
1. Each management trait has a value from 1 to 10 (1 being the least and 10 being the greatest). Circle the number you feel best indicates your level of strength or weakness in each trait.
2. After completing the survey, add the total score in each category and record your score on the line that says, "total score."

MANAGEMENT TRAITS ANALYSIS SURVEY

Rate yourself as to the extent the following characteristics represent you. Rate yourself on each characteristic with 10 being most like you and 1 being least like you.

A. The Promotional Manager

Outgoing, sociable	1 2 3 4 5 6 7 8 9 10
Inspires allegiance	1 2 3 4 5 6 7 8 9 10
Sincere	1 2 3 4 5 6 7 8 9 10
Positive attitude	1 2 3 4 5 6 7 8 9 10
Responsive to others	1 2 3 4 5 6 7 8 9 10
Talkative	1 2 3 4 5 6 7 8 9 10
Enthusiastic	1 2 3 4 5 6 7 8 9 10
Seldom worries	1 2 3 4 5 6 7 8 9 10
Compassionate	1 2 3 4 5 6 7 8 9 10
Generous	1 2 3 4 5 6 7 8 9 10
Undisciplined	1 2 3 4 5 6 7 8 9 10
Easily influenced	1 2 3 4 5 6 7 8 9 10
Restless	1 2 3 4 5 6 7 8 9 10
Disorganized	1 2 3 4 5 6 7 8 9 10
Undependable	1 2 3 4 5 6 7 8 9 10
Loud	1 2 3 4 5 6 7 8 9 10
Promotes self	1 2 3 4 5 6 7 8 9 10
Exaggerates	1 2 3 4 5 6 7 8 9 10
Fearful, insecure	1 2 3 4 5 6 7 8 9 10
Unproductive	1 2 3 4 5 6 7 8 9 10

Total Score _____

B. The Concept Manager

Natural talent	1	2	3	4	5	6	7	8	9	10
Analytical	1	2	3	4	5	6	7	8	9	10
Perfectionist	1	2	3	4	5	6	7	8	9	10
Conscientious	1	2	3	4	5	6	7	8	9	10
Loyal	1	2	3	4	5	6	7	8	9	10
Organized	1	2	3	4	5	6	7	8	9	10
Idealistic	1	2	3	4	5	6	7	8	9	10
Sensitive	1	2	3	4	5	6	7	8	9	10
Self-sacrificing	1	2	3	4	5	6	7	8	9	10
Self-disciplined	1	2	3	4	5	6	7	8	9	10
Moody	1	2	3	4	5	6	7	8	9	10
Negative	1	2	3	4	5	6	7	8	9	10
Critical	1	2	3	4	5	6	7	8	9	10
Resists change	1	2	3	4	5	6	7	8	9	10
Self-conscious	1	2	3	4	5	6	7	8	9	10
Unpredictable	1	2	3	4	5	6	7	8	9	10
Revengeful	1	2	3	4	5	6	7	8	9	10
Lacks self-confidence	1	2	3	4	5	6	7	8	9	10
Unsociable	1	2	3	4	5	6	7	8	9	10
Theoretical	1	2	3	4	5	6	7	8	9	10

Total Score _____

C. The Operational Manager

Determined	1	2	3	4	5	6	7	8	9	10
Independent	1	2	3	4	5	6	7	8	9	10
Productive	1	2	3	4	5	6	7	8	9	10
Decisive	1	2	3	4	5	6	7	8	9	10
Practical	1	2	3	4	5	6	7	8	9	10
Goal-oriented	1	2	3	4	5	6	7	8	9	10
Optimistic	1	2	3	4	5	6	7	8	9	10

Willing to risk	1	2	3	4	5	6	7	8	9	10
Self-confident	1	2	3	4	5	6	7	8	9	10
Willing to lead	1	2	3	4	5	6	7	8	9	10
Unsympathetic	1	2	3	4	5	6	7	8	9	10
Inconsiderate	1	2	3	4	5	6	7	8	9	10
Resists regulations	1	2	3	4	5	6	7	8	9	10
Cruel, sarcastic	1	2	3	4	5	6	7	8	9	10
Doesn't give recognition	1	2	3	4	5	6	7	8	9	10
Self-sufficient	1	2	3	4	5	6	7	8	9	10
Domineering	1	2	3	4	5	6	7	8	9	10
Opinionated	1	2	3	4	5	6	7	8	9	10
Proud	1	2	3	4	5	6	7	8	9	10
Cunning	1	2	3	4	5	6	7	8	9	10

Total Score _____

D. The Negotiating Manager

Calm, quiet	1	2	3	4	5	6	7	8	9	10
Easygoing	1	2	3	4	5	6	7	8	9	10
Likable	1	2	3	4	5	6	7	8	9	10
Diplomatic	1	2	3	4	5	6	7	8	9	10
Efficient, organized	1	2	3	4	5	6	7	8	9	10
Dependable, stable	1	2	3	4	5	6	7	8	9	10
Conservative	1	2	3	4	5	6	7	8	9	10
Practical	1	2	3	4	5	6	7	8	9	10
Reluctant leader	1	2	3	4	5	6	7	8	9	10
Dry humor	1	2	3	4	5	6	7	8	9	10
Unmotivated	1	2	3	4	5	6	7	8	9	10
Unexcitable	1	2	3	4	5	6	7	8	9	10
Avoids conflict	1	2	3	4	5	6	7	8	9	10
Spectator	1	2	3	4	5	6	7	8	9	10
Selfish	1	2	3	4	5	6	7	8	9	10
Stingy	1	2	3	4	5	6	7	8	9	10

Stubborn	1	2	3	4	5	6	7	8	9	10
Self-protective	1	2	3	4	5	6	7	8	9	10
Indecisive	1	2	3	4	5	6	7	8	9	10
Fear of risk	1	2	3	4	5	6	7	8	9	10

Total Score _____

PERSONAL PROFILE OF YOUR MANAGEMENT TRAITS

After totaling the score in each of the four management trait categories, you are now ready to begin developing a personal profile of your management traits on figure 5 on page 84.

Instructions

Review your management trait survey and then record on the form in figure five each management trait receiving a score of 7 or more. Place an X in the score column corresponding with the score of each trait being listed. Your management traits survey consists of all of your management traits receiving a score of 7 or more, regardless of their management trait classification.

Management trait "Dominators" are those traits receiving a score of 7–8. These traits tend to dominate the "weaker" traits in a particular classification or category. The management trait "Regulators" are those traits receiving a score of 9–10. They represent the strongest drive in one's makeup, and provide the greatest input toward how the manager acts or reacts in a given situation.

PERSONAL PROFILE OF YOUR
MANAGEMENT TRAITS

MANAGEMENT TRAITS	DOMINATORS		REGULATORS	
	7	8	9	10

Figure 5: This form is designed to help identify your profile of management traits.

HOW YOU RATED YOURSELF ON THE SURVEY

Now that you have scored the results and completed the "Personal Profile of Your Management Traits," let's look at how you rated yourself.

Turn back to each category (A, B, C, D) and look at how you scored yourself. Now find the category receiving the highest and second highest scores.

If category C, the Operational manager, received the highest score, then you will identify more closely with the traits listed in that category. If your second highest score was B, the Concept manager, you would also be able to recognize yourself in many of the traits listed in that category.

However, the category in which you scored the highest isn't nearly as important to you as the traits listed in the "Personal Profile of Your Management Traits." Look again at figure 5 and determine how many of those traits are considered weaknesses and how many strengths.

Next, notice how many are "dominators" and "regulators." The regulators cut across all category lines and tend to be very evident regardless of the classification receiving the highest score.

For example, let's suppose your highest score was classification A, the Promotional manager. Normally promotional managers are not perfectionists. However, if you scored a 9 or 10 in the perfectionistic trait in category B (the concept manager), that trait is so strong it will have a "regulating" effect on the promotional management category. On the other hand, if you had only scored a 7 in perfectionist, people could still see that characteristic in you, but it would not be strong enough to cut across category lines and regulate other management types.

The traits listed in the "Personal Profile of Your Management Traits" are the ones more important in developing your management potential. They represent the strongest traits from each of the four categories and will have the greatest influence on you as a manager or leader.

Using the forms shown in figures 6 and 7 on pages 86–87, record those traits that you consider strengths and weaknesses, as listed on the "Personal Profile of Your Management Traits" form. To

PERSONAL PROFILE OF YOUR MANAGEMENT TRAIT
STRENGTHS

TRAITS CONSIDERED STRENGTHS	DOMINATORS	REGULATORS

Figure 6: Use this form to record your management traits that you consider to be strengths.

PERSONAL PROFILE OF YOUR MANAGEMENT TRAIT
WEAKNESSES

TRAITS CONSIDERED WEAKNESSES	DOMINATORS	REGULATORS

Figure 7: Use this form to record your management traits that you consider to be weaknesses.

more effectively develop your potential as a manager you must begin focusing on how to capitalize on your strengths and overcome or minimize your weaknesses. This process will be discussed in detail later.

HOW TO USE THIS SURVEY

This survey is not intended to be a personality or psychological test. It is simply a survey of the type of traits that tend to impact a person's day-to-day management actions and reactions. Therefore, do not attempt to use it to test personality or psychological characteristics.

However, this survey can be extremely beneficial in assisting with the development of your management potential. Very few leaders and managers ever take the time to find out the effect of their management traits on their careers. And yet, management traits play a major role in shaping one's career as a leader. Thus, the information learned from this survey should not be taken lightly.

Correctly identifying traits that help or hinder one's development as a manager, and then capitalizing on the strengths and minimizing the weaknesses may do more to advance your career than any other single thing you do. Your development as a manager will be in direct proportion to your development as a person.

You may find it helpful to have another person who knows you well (such as a mate, family member, or close associate at work) take the test giving their view of how you score on each line item. When both of you have completed the test, compare the results trait by trait. This will help you compare your view of your strengths and weaknesses with others who know you well.

When using this survey, keep the following points clearly in mind:

1. *Different traits are needed in different jobs.* During management seminars and consulting sessions I am frequently asked if there is a universal set of traits that make up the profile of the highly productive and successful manager. The answer is no. There are traits that are absolutely essential for any manager or leader to be successful. However, we must keep in mind that different

types of jobs require different types of traits.

For example, it is much more essential for a surgeon to be a perfectionist than for a salesperson. People in sales and public relations work need to develop and cultivate more of the traits found in category A, the Promotional manager, than people working in research and development. People in research and development careers will need to acquire more of the traits found in category B, the Concept manager.

As you progress in your career as a manager, the type of job you have will determine the type of traits you need to cultivate and develop. You will discover that traits that are extremely beneficial in one type of job are not necessarily important in another. In fact, some traits considered beneficial in one type of job may actually become detrimental in another.

2. *One management category is neither better nor worse than another.* The traits of the Negotiating manager are neither better nor worse than those found in the Promotional manager. Therefore, don't think you need to switch categories. You will find that you need to develop some of the traits found in other categories, but Operational managers are just as important and needed as Concept managers.

In fact, to achieve their full potential, most organizations need all four types of managers represented. Promotional managers are needed in sales and public relations departments; Concept managers are needed in research and development positions; Operational managers are needed in production areas; and Negotiating managers are needed to deal with legal matters, and handle conflicts and negotiate contracts.

The important thing is to make sure you have the right person with the right traits in the right job at the right time. The manager or organization that accomplishes that is well on the way to achieving success.

3. *Maintain balance when focusing on strengths and weaknesses.* As you work to improve your strengths and minimize your weaknesses, keep reminding yourself that you need to do both. It is just as important to keep developing your strengths as it is to reduce your weaknesses. To achieve one without the other will not necessarily make you a better manager; in fact, it may greatly limit

your potential in this strategic area.

For example, if you spend all of your time trying to overcome your weaknesses you will be neglecting your strengths. And if you neglect your strengths, your performance and productivity will suffer. On the other hand, if you spend all of your time improving your areas of strength, your weaknesses will become even greater.

4. *When dealing with traits you are also dealing with habits.* As you work to improve strengths and reduce weaknesses, keep in mind you are not only dealing with traits, but habits as well. People who are undisciplined tend to develop a habit of being late to meetings and appointments. Therefore, you aren't just dealing with a trait, you are also dealing with the habits that have been formed because of the traits.

That is why it takes time to cultivate new traits and get rid of old ones. You make a decision to become more decisive, but you will find that just making that decision will not automatically make you a more decisive person. You will also have to break the habit of procrastination you have developed over the years. And breaking old habits and replacing them with new ones always takes time.

Do not become discouraged as you work at developing your strengths and reducing your weaknesses, because it will take time. However, it is the best investment of your time you can make. As you develop your strengths and overcome your weaknesses you are evolving as a person as well as a manager.

PERSONAL APPLICATION

1. Fill out the Management Traits Analysis Survey in this chapter.
2. Have someone else fill out the survey evaluating your traits from their perspective.
3. Compare your perception of your traits with their perception. How are they different? How are they alike? What do you learn from this?
4. Complete the form in Figure 5 on page 84.
5. Next complete the forms shown in figures 6 and 7 on pages 86–87.
6. Begin developing an action plan as to how you will improve in

your areas of strengths and minimize your areas of weaknesses. (Take one or two strengths and weaknesses at a time to work on.)

7. Ask someone to hold you accountable for accomplishing this.
8. Meet with that person periodically to evaluate your progress.

7

YOUR MANAGEMENT TRAITS IN ACTION

In the last chapter you were given an opportunity to take the Management Traits Analysis Survey. You should not read this chapter until you have completed assignments 1–5 of the "Personal Application" section at the end of chapter 6.

This chapter deals with your management traits in action. It covers the four management categories listed in the Management Traits Analysis Survey, explaining how each type of manager tends to function in light of his or her personal strengths and weaknesses.

The following descriptions of the four types of managers are given in general terms. No one possesses 100 percent of the traits in any given category. We are all a mixture, to varying degrees, of all four, as the "Personal Profile of Your Management Traits" form indicates once it is completed.

However, as you read the descriptions of the four types of managers you will be able to see yourself, as well as others you know, and you will begin to understand why people act and react the way they do in various management situations.

TRAITS OF THE PROMOTIONAL MANAGER

The Promotional manager tends to possess the following traits:
- Outgoing, sociable
- Inspires allegiance
- Sincere
- Positive attitude
- Responsive to others
- Talkative
- Undisciplined
- Easily influenced
- Restless
- Disorganized
- Undependable
- Loud

- Enthusiastic
- Seldom worries
- Compassionate
- Generous

- Promotes self
- Exaggerates
- Fearful, Insecure
- Unproductive

As with all four types of managers, the Promotional manager contains traits that represent both strengths and weaknesses. In fact, any strength carried to an extreme can become a weakness. For example, "enthusiastic" is one of the Promotional manager's strengths. However, enthusiasm carried too far can lead to exaggeration, one of the Promotional manager's weaknesses.

Let's look at the group of traits classified as the type we will call the Promotional manager, and examine how each trait tends to impact the day-to-day actions and reactions to this type of manager.

Outgoing, sociable. The Promotional manager is a people person. Such managers are at their best when working with people. In fact, they tend to need people and the support and protection they feel when working with them. The Promotional manager makes friends quickly, is also easy to talk to, and as a result is usually well liked by other employees, especially those not working directly for him or her.

Inspires allegiance. The Promotional manager is not only outgoing and sociable, but also has the ability to inspire allegiance from others. This trait aids in selling ideas to others. In fact, this type of person has the traits necessary to become an excellent salesperson. Promotional managers can motivate others, especially for a short period of time, to follow their leadership. And that is an important quality for any manager or leader to have.

Sincere. This type of manager is a very sincere person. As a result of this trait people tend to trust the Promotional manager who, in turn, tends to trust others. Such sincerity is very believable. That is one of the reasons this type of person does so well in sales or public relations work.

Positive attitude. The Promotional manager doesn't know the meaning of the words, "I can't." He always sees the best in people and frequently gives his employees verbal praise. An eternal optimist, he believes the future will be better than the past, and has great faith that whatever plans he and his people develop will be achieved.

93

Responsive to others. It is not difficult for the Promotional manager to adopt the philosophy that the manager's job is to serve the needs of others. As a result, people tend to seek out this type of manager because they know he or she will listen and attempt to meet their needs.

However, this strength carried to extremes tends to become a weakness. And as a result, the Promotional manager usually has great difficulty saying no to people, even when he should. This creates great problems because the Promotional manager's inability to say no causes him to overcommit himself. He also tends to allow subordinates to delegate work and decisions up to him instead of delegating down to subordinates.

This trait also tends to cause the manager to seek popularity. And oftentimes it is more important to him to be known as a "good guy" than to make the hard management decisions that need to be made. He continually is drawn to be more concerned with people, their feelings, and well-being than he is about productivity.

Talkative. This frequently creates communication problems, because he would much rather hear himself talk than listen to the thoughts and ideas of others.

His talkative nature also becomes a major time waster. His coffee and lunch breaks tend to frequently go far beyond the allotted time simply because he enjoys talking with people. He is the type of manager that can stick his head in your office and say, "Have you got a minute?" An hour later he is still talking and seemingly unaware he is keeping people from their work.

Enthusiastic. If you need some enthusiasm injected into the meeting, call on this manager. She tends to be enthusiastic about everything she does, and usually about the things you are doing as well. This is a very important trait, and it's one of the reasons the Promotional manager is able to inspire allegiance and motivate people to action. She is not only enthusiastic, but is usually able to create enthusiasm in others as well. This is why many people enjoy working with, for, and around this manager.

Seldom worries. The Promotional manager tends to be able to handle pressure well. In fact, it usually is difficult to make him or her feel under pressure. He seldom worries, choosing instead to look on the positive side of things. As a result, he is one of the last people to give up on an idea, even when it isn't working. He always seems to have faith in himself and those around him, believing things will always work out for the best.

Compassionate. He is able to feel with people when they hurt and laugh with them when they are happy. This is a trait that more managers need to develop; however, it also creates lots of problems for the Promotional manager when carried too far. For example, his compassion frequently causes him to overcommit to things, make promises he can't fulfill, overlook faults and problems in others when he should be confronting them, and become excessively concerned with feelings rather than facts or performance.

Generous. He will give you the shirt off his back, if someone else hasn't gotten it first. This is one of the reasons it is easy for him to serve the needs of his people. He enjoys doing things for others, especially if he feels appreciated for his efforts.

However, again this strength carried to extremes becomes a weakness. The Promotional manager frequently finds himself compromising or giving in to the demands or requests of others when he should be saying no. His generous attitude allows people to take advantage of him and get away with things that would not be allowed by other types of managers.

Undisciplined. This is one of the Promotional manager's greatest weaknesses. We have seen some of his great strengths, but this weakness frequently undermines many of those strengths. He has a great deal of difficulty managing his time effectively. He is great at coming up with creative plans, but he is terrible at following through and seeing the project to completion. This manager tends to hate detail and routines. He is quick to make a commitment to someone, but then frequently fails to keep it. He has a great deal of difficulty keeping on schedule and frequently misses deadlines. In fact, he hates deadlines!

Easily influenced. As a result, she sometimes appears to lack strong convictions of her own. She does have strong conviction; however, it is easy for people to sell her on a different idea or plan. She tends to operate more out of emotions and feelings than on facts. She will use facts to support her emotions; however, it is easy for her to ignore facts in favor of feelings. This sometimes

95

causes her to make poor judgments and bad decisions.

Restless. It is easy for him to become excited about a project, but he quickly tires of it, seeking something new and different to excite and motivate him again. He tends to be an excellent project "start-up person," but once it is up and running he quickly becomes bored and needs a new project to start. He is not a maintainer. He constantly is looking for new challenges and projects to work on, but it doesn't seem to bother him to leave them before they are completed.

Disorganized. The Promotional manager's desk and office is usually a mess. He has problems keeping his day organized. It is difficult for him to develop a schedule and stick with it. He also tends to think more in terms of generalities than in detail. He would much rather leave filling in the details to someone else.

Undependable. The Promotional manager tends to have difficulty following through with his commitments, and he overextends himself. He may tell you he will meet you at 2:30, but then forget the meeting while having an extended coffee break.

This type of manager tends to function from the perspective of "out of sight, out of mind." He doesn't intentionally neglect meetings, but other things come up and he can easily get involved with others.

Loud. At times the Promotional manager can be very overbearing. Be forewarned because in his enthusiasm he can become very loud and boisterous.

Promotes self. She also spends an excessive amount of time talking about herself, her accomplishments, ideas, feelings, and opinions.

Exaggerates. Because he is so enthusiastic, the Promotional manager tends to exaggerate the facts at times. Things usually are never quite as good or bad as he presents them as being. Because of this, some people feel he can't be trusted. However, in most cases his exaggerations aren't necessarily intentional; he just gets carried away with his descriptions.

Fearful, insecure. Even though he is an extrovert, in most cases his actions and outgoing nature are efforts to cover up his own insecurities with himself. He tends to lack confidence in himself, but compensates by his positive, outgoing and warm interaction with people. He attempts to put others at ease in an effort to become at ease with himself.

Unproductive. The Promotional manager is very activity oriented, but should be a lot more productive based on the efforts and energies he expends. Most of this is due to his undisciplined and disorganized daily routine. He is generally overextended with commitments to help others, and in the process doesn't get his own work accomplished.

As you can see, the Promotional manager has some great strengths, but also some glaring weaknesses. And we will see that same pattern in the remaining three types: the Concept manager, the Operational manager, and the Negotiating manager.

If your highest score was in category A, the Promotional manager, then you need to continue to develop your strengths, but begin at once working on your weaknesses. Your greatest problems evolve around lack of discipline and organization. Work on these first, because you will never experience your full management potential until you overcome these negative traits. There are plentiful tools and aids on the market today to help the manager in these problem areas. Pick those that best suit your needs and begin the habit of using them on a daily basis.

No matter what type of trait you are working on, be it a strength or a weakness, the key is making a commitment and being consistent in its application. At that time, it will become a trait contributing to, instead of hindering, the development of your managerial potential.

TRAITS OF THE CONCEPT MANAGER

The Concept manager tends to have the following management traits:

- Natural talent
- Analytical
- Perfectionist
- Conscientious
- Loyal
- Organized
- Idealistic
- Moody
- Negative
- Critical
- Resists change
- Self-conscious
- Unpredictable
- Revengeful

- Sensitive
- Self-sacrificing
- Self-disciplined
- Lacks self-confidence
- Unsociable
- Theoretical

As with all other types discussed in this chapter, the Concept manager has some great and extremely important strengths; however, he also has some very serious weaknesses.

Natural talent. He or she usually is very smart and tends to possess a considerable amount of natural ability and skill. Anything the Concept manager does is usually done better than others because of the numerous strengths possessed.

Analytical. The Concept manager is usually very analytical. She has great capacity and patience to study a situation from every angle before making a decision. She tends to investigate every possibility and usually doesn't overlook a single detail.

Perfectionist. I'm sure it was a Concept manager who first coined the phrase, "If it's worth doing, it's worth doing right!" This attitude is a driving and consuming force in everything the Concept manager does, from the way work on a desk is arranged to the planning of every detail of a major project.

He or she is always striving for perfection. However, such managers are never quite satisfied with the results, no matter how good they may be. They tend to always think things could and should be done better. As a result, they are generally much harder on themselves and others than they should be.

And unlike the Promotional manager, the Concept manager has difficulty giving verbal praise to others, because of never being quite satisfied with a performance, and always thinking of ways it could and should have been done better. Even though this is a great strength, carried to an extreme it makes working with and for such a manager difficult at times.

Conscientious. Perfectionist and conscientious traits go hand in hand. Usually where you find one, you will also find the other. The Concept manager is greatly concerned with all aspects of his work. He is especially concerned about doing what he says he will do, and he has little patience with those who don't follow through. That is one of the reasons why there is so much potential for conflict between the Concept and Promotional managers. The Concept manager sees the Promotional manager as being very undependable (a trait he or she can't tolerate).

Loyal. The Concept manager will be true to his commitments, see the project through to the end, and stick with you through both good and bad times. He tends to be very committed to supporting those he works for, and does not generally hide things from people. If he is working under a contract, he can usually be counted on to fulfill it to the letter.

Organized. Unlike the Promotional manager, the Concept manager is one of the most organized people you will ever meet. The traits of being analytical, perfectionistic, and organized tend to make the Concept manager a good administrator. She is highly organized personally and great at organizing jobs and activities for others. However, she is very poor at motivating others to do the job once it is organized.

Idealistic. This is a great strength, but carried to extremes it becomes a serious weakness. He is always thinking in terms of what should be, and that becomes his goal. Unfortunately what should be and what has to be are sometimes miles apart. As a result some of the things the Concept manager wants to do are not very practical.

Sensitive. The Concept manager's feelings can be hurt very easily, and he is always worrying about how he is being perceived. This can become a serious problem because of his perfectionist trait. He is never satisfied with his own performance; therefore, he automatically assumes others aren't either. However, people usually are trying to give him far more credit and recognition than he feels he deserves.

Self-sacrificing. Both the Concept and Promotional managers tend to be self-sacrificing, but for different reasons. The Promotional manager tends to give of himself because it makes him feel good. On the other hand, the Concept manager usually gives of himself because of a sense of obligation.

Self-disciplined. By this time it is probably becoming apparent that in many respects the Promotional and Concept managers are almost exact opposites. The Concept manager is very disciplined while the Promotional one is extremely undisciplined. The Concept person tends to be in control of himself and his emotions at all times, but the Promotional manager is usually guided by his emotions. As a result, as his emotions change, he changes. But the Concept manager tries to keep his emotions from controlling him. Rather than operate on emotion, he tends to operate on reason and logic.

Moody. Even though the Concept manager works hard at operating out of logic rather than emotion, he is a very emotional person. In fact, he frequently experiences great mood swings. He can be on top of the world when he comes to work in the morning, but if things don't go right he can experience great depression. This is partly due to the fact of how hard he is on himself, never quite measuring up to his own expectations and requirements.

Negative. The Concept manager's perfectionist trait tends to contribute to his frequent negative attitudes. These negative attitudes frequently become a great source of conflict between him and the Promotional manager. While the Promotional manager tends to believe all of his ideas are good and workable, the Concept manager's first reaction to a new idea is usually negative. He automatically looks for all the reasons why ideas won't work.

Critical. It is very difficult for the Concept manager to praise others because of his perfectionist trait. He tends to never be satisfied with results. He usually looks for areas that could and should have been done better, rather than give people credit for what they have done.

Resists change. The Concept manager prefers to stick with those traditions that have proven themselves to be reliable. She resists change because it involves risk-taking. Risks can lead to failure and her perfectionist attitude deplores failure.

Rather than try something new, the Concept manager would rather perfect what has already been established as working. As a result, she tends to be very conservative during her planning process.

Self-conscious. He is always worrying about what others think of him. He is far more critical of himself than others are of him. People tend to greatly admire his ability and accomplishment, but he is never satisfied with them.

Unpredictable. Even though the Concept manager resists change, he is unpredictable because of his continuous mood changes. You never know what kind of mood he will be in, or what may happen to change his mood.

Revengeful. The Concept manager never forgets when he is wronged, and his analytical and perfectionist mind becomes a real asset when he decides to get even. It is very hard for him to forgive and forget when someone crosses him.

Lacks self-confidence. He is a very talented and productive person, but he has very little confidence in his ability. His first reaction tends to be, "Oh, I could never do that!" However, in most instances he can do the job better than anyone else, but he will almost never volunteer. On the other hand, the Promotional manager is usually the first to volunteer, but can't do the job as well as his Concept counterpart.

Unsociable. Unlike the Promotional manager, the Concept person is very unsociable. He is an introvert by nature and avoids people whenever he can. He would much rather be left alone to perfect the various functions of his project than have to work with people.

Theoretical. The Concept manager tends to deal with the theoretical rather than the practical. She would rather research all the information, gather all the facts, and study the situation from all the angles than actually do the job.

TRAITS OF THE OPERATIONAL MANAGER

The Operational manager tends to have the following management traits:

- Determined
- Independent
- Productive
- Decisive
- Practical
- Goal-oriented
- Optimistic
- Willing to risk
- Self-confident
- Willing to lead
- Unsympathetic
- Inconsiderate
- Resists regulations
- Cruel, sarcastic
- Doesn't give recognition
- Self-sufficient
- Domineering
- Opinionated
- Proud
- Cunning

Determined. The Operational manager doesn't know the meaning of the words, "I can't," or "That won't work!" In fact, if someone tells him he can't do something or make something work, he will break his back in an effort to prove that person wrong.

Independent. The Operational manager tends to be a loner. He is very independent, not easily swayed from his beliefs and convictions, and doesn't need people to get a job done. He would rather do it himself than take the time to show someone else how it should be done.

Productive. He may not do the job the way you would do it, and he certainly won't do the job the way the Concept manager would do it, but he will get the job done one way or the other. He tends to be much more concerned with "quantity" than "quality," which is just the opposite of the Concept person.

Decisive. Decision-making comes easy for him. His attitude is, "Let's try it, it might work." And if it doesn't work, then he simply tries something else until he finds a solution.

He can make a decision and solve a problem before the Concept manager has located all of the sources he tends to use in gathering research and data to evaluate, or before the Promotional manager is even aware there was a problem in the first place. Granted, his decisions are not always the best, but his attitude is, "If this doesn't work, we'll simply try something else."

Practical. The Operational manager avoids theoretical issues and simply tries to find out what works without concerning himself with the reasons why. He takes a very logical approach to planning and the implementation of those plans. He wants to know how to get the most done with the least amount of cost and effort. That tends to be the motivating factor behind all his decisions.

Goal-oriented. She is also a very goal-oriented person. In fact, she is driven by goals. She must have a goal to work toward every day. And the accomplishment of that goal becomes all important, even more important than how well she did in the process of getting there.

The only time the Operational manager tends to get depressed is when she isn't working on and achieving several goals. Since she is so goal-oriented, it is easy for her to expect and require her subordinates to have measurable goals as well.

Optimistic. The Operational manager, like the Promotional manager, is a positive thinker. However, the Operational manager is positive because he has a proven track record of results. He believes in himself and his ability, and that is the source of his optimistic outlook. He doesn't necessarily have a great deal of confidence in others, but he believes there is nothing he can't do.

Willing to risk. He thrives on the challenge of the risk. The greater the risk involved, the harder he works to insure his success.

Self-confident. He has a proven track record of success that serves to feed his self-confidence. He tends to draw his opinion and image of himself from his achievements. Therefore, he has a very high regard for himself and what he is able to do.

Willing to lead. Most people would call the Operational manager a "natural leader." However, as we will soon see, that couldn't be further from the truth. He winds up being the leader because while others are seeking the goal, he has the job completed because he knows what needs to be done and isn't afraid to make the decisions necessary in accomplishing the goal.

He is going to be the "leader" whether people ask him to or not. But he isn't necessarily a good leader because he views people as being in the way of getting the job done. Followers are just a necessary evil to be put up with in getting the job done.

Unsympathetic. The Operational manager tends to be very unsympathetic to the needs, concerns, and feelings of others. People become expendable in light of accomplishing the goal. As a result, such a manager tends to use people, and take from people, but gives back very little in return.

Inconsiderate. She tends to think about what is best for her and the accomplishment of her goals and rarely, if ever, considers what is best for others. As a result, she has a great deal of difficulty serving the needs of her subordinates, but she certainly expects and demands that they serve her needs.

Resists regulations. The Operational manager has a great deal of difficulty following and complying with regulations. As a result, he frequently has trouble working within the confines of an organizational structure. He learns to manipulate the system to accomplish his own goals and purposes.

That is why many Operational managers finally go into business for themselves. They continually find themselves at odds with the organization and its rules and regulations and frequently wind up leaving. However, once they are in charge, they usually develop just as many policies and procedures and are just as insistent that others follow them as the leaders of the organization they left.

Operational managers have a great need to be in control, and organizational regulations limit their freedom of movement and control. Therefore, they continually resist and fight against controls and regulations.

Cruel, sarcastic. Such cruelty is more in the form of verbal abuse than physical. He can make cutting remarks that hurt deeply and not even realize how his words have affected people. As a result, the Operational manager tends to have difficulty inspiring allegiance and motivating subordinates. Those who do follow him usually do so more out of fear than anything else.

Doesn't give recognition. The attitude is: "I'm paying you to do the job right. Therefore, I shouldn't have to give you any special recognition for work properly done, because that is your job. And if you don't do the job right, you'll hear about it from me."

Most of the recognition the Operational manager gives is in the form of criticism for mistakes made, but he rarely, if ever, compliments people for jobs well done.

Self-sufficient. The Operational person doesn't need help from others; therefore, she rarely asks for assistance. She knows how she wants the job done and would rather do it herself than ask for help. As a result, she tends to be very poor at teaching others. She knows how to do the job, but she doesn't know how to train others to do it.

Domineering. He tends to use an authoritative style of leadership and usually retains most of the decision-making power. He usually doesn't trust others, and if people misuse authority he is quick to take it back.

Opinionated. The Operational manager has his own ideas for getting things done, and therefore, rarely asks for input from others. And when input is given, he uses only those ideas that agree with his own.

Proud. He takes a great deal of pride in the fact that he can get things done, and he doesn't like to have his views, opinions, and ideas challenged.

Cunning. The Operational manager is very committed to his own goals and objectives. He knows how he wants things done, and he is able to find every loophole in the rules that may stand in his way. This manager has the ability to manipulate people and events to suit his own needs and interests.

TRAITS OF THE NEGOTIATING MANAGER

The Negotiating manager tends to have the following traits:

- Calm, quiet
- Easygoing
- Likable
- Diplomatic
- Efficient, organized
- Dependable, stable
- Conservative
- Practical
- Reluctant leader
- Dry humor
- Unmotivated
- Unexcitable
- Avoids conflict
- Spectator
- Selfish
- Stingy
- Stubborn
- Self-protective
- Indecisive
- Fear of risk

Calm, quiet. Nothing ever seems to bother the Negotiating manager. Even during the pressure created by a crisis, he is able to keep his emotions on an even keel. He is able to remain emotionally calm when facing important issues and decisions. That helps him keep things in proper perspective and make better decisions.

Easygoing. She is very easygoing and easy to be around. People enjoy working with and around her much more than the Operational manager.

Likable. The Negotiating manager has very few enemies. He is good-natured and generally liked by most people, both subordinates as well as supervisors.

Diplomatic. Negotiating managers are able to consider all points of view and then make the correct decision. They try to avoid personal conflicts, but are very good at helping others successfully solve their differences. As a result, people frequently seek them out for advice on problems.

Efficient, organized. The Negotiating manager doesn't do things with a lot of pomp and flare. He is very thorough and does all of his work efficiently and effectively. And all the while, he avoids the limelight, even though he probably deserves the greatest amount of recognition.

Dependable, stable. Like the Concept manager, he is a person of his word. If he tells you a report will be on your desk at 10 o'clock Thursday morning, you can relax, because it will be there. He always follows through with what he commits to do, and he is always there when he is needed.

The Negotiating person is a stabilizing force in the organization. He doesn't get involved in every new fad or philosophy that comes along in the midst of a changing environment.

Conservative. He is a very conservative person, both financially and in his value system. In fact, you frequently find this type of manager heading up the finance department in many organizations. He is happiest when he is able to avoid spending money, or when he can find a good bargain. "Cheap" tends to be more important to him than "quality."

He usually keeps to the middle of the road on most issues, and rarely favors rapid change. In fact, if he had his way things would stay much the way they are, as long as they are going well. He doesn't want anything or anyone to rock the boat. But when change comes he is usually able to adapt more quickly and effectively than any other type of manager.

Practical. Like the Operational manager, he is a very practical person. He is much more interested in what works than how good something looks.

Reluctant leader. He has great leadership skills, but he will never volunteer to be the leader. However, people frequently would much rather follow the Negotiating manager than the Operational one, but they rarely get the chance.

Dry humor. She is not loud and jolly like the Promotional manager. But she has a great sense of dry humor. Most of her humor is shared with a straight face, and you may not even know she is telling a joke. Her sense of humor helps people relax during tense situations, and she seems to know exactly when to inject humor into a situation.

Unmotivated. Lack of motivation is one of Negotiating managers' greatest weaknesses. They need deadlines and someone to hold them accountable, or else they can become very unproductive. They rarely, if ever, volunteer, but if you ask them for help they will do a very good job.

Unexcitable. He rarely gets excited about anything and seldom worries. In fact, there are times he should become more excited and concerned than he is. As a result, he frequently fails to hold subordinates accountable for important things that should be completed in a timely manner.

Avoids conflict. The Negotiating manager will go to great lengths to avoid a personal conflict. He would rather someone take advantage of him than start a conflict. This trait allows people like the Operational manager to take advantage of him. But even when that occurs, he tends to remain calm.

Spectator. He is more a spectator than a player. However, his diplomatic skills make him a very valuable member on a management team. He is usually the one that winds up negotiating compromises when the Promotional, Concept, and Operational managers find themselves deadlocked in a serious conflict.

Selfish. He tends to be very self-centered, attempting to continually manipulate situations in his favor. He wants to keep what he has earned and generally isn't free in sharing his ideas or the secrets of his success.

Stingy. He is also very tight with money. His goal is to keep what he has earned, and he frequently misses out on opportunities because he is unwilling to part with the money required to make the investment. His philosophy is, "A bird in the hand is worth two in the bush," and he consistently lives by that formula.

Stubborn. Once she makes up her mind, she can be very stubborn. She can help others compromise, but she can be very unbending when pushed or backed into a corner.

Self-protective. The Negotiating manager's primary concern is self-preservation. He or she is very protective of personal time and space and tends to be a very private person.

Indecisive. The lack of decision doesn't seem to bother him. This trait frustrates the Operational manager personality to no end, and that is one of the major reasons these two management types don't get along if a Negotiating manager is supervising an Operational one.

The Negotiating type isn't indecisive because he doesn't know what decision to make, but because he doesn't place as much importance on making the decision in a timely manner.

Fear of risk. The Negotiating manager does not like to take risks. He is very uncomfortable with the unknown and works best in stable, traditional surroundings. He wants to avoid surprises and is usually not a good gambler.

QUESTIONS I AM MOST FREQUENTLY ASKED

During seminars and consulting sessions I am frequently asked a variety of questions regarding traits that help or hinder a manager's development. You may have some of the same questions; therefore, I will address some of the ones most frequently asked.

Are some traits more important than others in the development of one's potential as a manager? The answer is yes. For example, the further you advance in your management career the more important people skills become.

When you first begin your management skills, say as a first-line supervisor, technical skills are very important. You should be a specialist in your field. That is, you should have a thorough understanding of the various skills, duties, and functions your subordinates are required to perform. You need to be knowledgeable of the jobs to be performed by your people on a day-to-day basis and the skill level needed to perform those tasks. You are supervising technicians; therefore, you need to have been a technician yourself to effectively supervise your people, properly plan with them, and correctly evaluate the results.

However, the further up the management ladder you advance your technical skills become less important while your people skills become more necessary. You must become a generalist instead of a specialist. Learn how to become a team player and then a team leader.

As you manage more people there is more demand on your time. So you must become better organized, disciplined, and capable of effectively managing your time. Always remember: The more control you have over an organization, the more control you must have over yourself. To become a good manager of an organization you first must become a good manager of yourself.

How do I develop a plan for improving my strengths and overcoming my weaknesses? First, fill out the Management Traits Analysis Survey, following the steps described in chapter 6. To develop your strengths and overcome your weaknesses you first must know what they are.

Second, don't try to do it all at once. Work on one or two areas at a time. Talk to other managers you respect, who have developed that strength or overcome that weakness and ask them for input. You can also benefit from topical books and articles in your interest areas.

Third, set "action goals" for yourself. Don't just develop head knowledge, but determine what you will actually *do* in developing a strength or overcoming a weakness. This is accomplished through specific actions. It isn't enough to just read something on the subject or talk to people about the problem. Nothing positive will happen until you begin taking specific action.

Fourth, keep in mind you will never overcome all your weaknesses. Don't become consumed by focusing on your weaknesses. It is far better to focus on developing strengths. Then find someone who is strong where you are weak and let them assist you in that area. Keep in mind that if you spend all your time eliminating weaknesses your strengths will be neglected. Your greatest potential lies in focusing on your strengths.

On what strengths and weaknesses should I be working? The answer varies from person to person. However, there are some fundamental traits that are critical to the development of every manager's potential, regardless of the type of business or organization you are working in.

Every manager needs to become strong in the following areas:

- Responsiveness to others
- Ability to inspire allegiance
- Self-discipline
- Decision-making skills
- Becoming goal-oriented
- Organization
- Self-confidence
- Diplomacy
- Being a team player
- Developing a positive outlook

This is only a sample list. You should look at your own position and decide those traits that are most critical to your performance. Then, begin working on the traits that will best prepare you to properly perform your responsibilities. Once you have accomplished that, begin working on the traits needed for advancing in your career.

Keep in mind that your personal development is a never ending process. You will never "arrive." There will always be areas of strength and weakness to be working on. Your commitment to development as a person is the most important decision you can make as you strive to develop your management potential.

PERSONAL APPLICATION

1. What have you learned about yourself in reading this chapter?
2. Do you have a clearer understanding of the traits on which you need to be working?
3. How can you use the information in the past two chapters to begin helping others to develop their potential?
4. Continue working on the assignments given at the end of chapter 6.

8

LEADING VS. MANAGING

Your potential as a manager depends, to a large extent, on your ability as a leader. You may have excellent management skills, but you can never reach your full potential as a manager until you also become an excellent leader. Management is something you do. Whereas a leader is something you are. It is possible to be an excellent leader, but a poor manager. And it is also possible to have excellent management skills but not know how to lead.

Jack Dillard held a middle management position for a large Christian organization. I first met Jack while conducting management training and consulting work for his organization in Southeast Asia. Jack was an excellent manager, but he was greatly lacking in leadership skills.

While I was conducting a role clarification session with the executive leadership team, Jack's name came up as a possible candidate for filling an upper management position. During the lunch break Jack's supervisor came up to me and said, "Myron, I just don't feel Jack has the qualifications to fill the position. He is a very good manager, but he lacks the skills needed to effectively lead a team of strong individuals like himself."

Dan Archeletta, Jack's supervisor, explained that Jack had advanced very rapidly through the ranks of management because he had good administrative skills. Jack was very organized, could set goals and get them accomplished, and was able to get a lot of work out of his people. However, he didn't get along well with people.

Dan explained, "He is a very authoritative individual, and he gets a lot accomplished within his department, but people do their jobs because they are intimidated by Jack, not because they are motivated. In this position the people Jack would be supervising

111

won't be easily intimidated, nor will they respond positively to his authoritative attitude. He would have to be able to motivate them as a team leader, and I just don't think he knows how to do that."

I later spent an entire evening with Jack Dillard. Jack's military training had prepared him to handle most administrative duties on his job. He thrived on a challenge, knew how to set goals and get them accomplished, and he maintained high performance standards, both for himself and his subordinates. "I'm here to get a job done," he said. "People who work for me learn how to do the job the way I expect, or they don't stay around long."

Jack quoted Colossians 3:23 as his justification for using whatever means necessary to maintain high levels of performance. He demanded high performance from everyone who worked for him. "I admit I may not be the most popular manager in the organization," he said with a smile, "but I get as much done as anyone else around here, and I get more accomplished than most. And after all, results is what we're after!"

It was obvious Dan Archeletta's concerns were well-founded. Jack did have good administrative skills. He knew how to get performance out of people, but he obviously would not do well as the team leader of top-level managers who would be neither impressed nor intimidated by Jack's approach. Jack had proven himself to be a good manager, but he had a long way to go before qualifying as a top executive.

LEADING AND MANAGING: THE DIFFERENCE

Management consists of those tasks and functions we perform in the coordination and utilization of resources to accomplish a specific objective. Leadership consists of those tasks and functions we perform to recruit, motivate, and influence others to follow us in the pursuit of a goal.

Leadership deals with the motivation and unification of people toward a common cause, goal, or objective. However, management deals with the effective utilization of all resources, time, materials, money, and manpower to accomplish a predetermined result in the most efficient and effective way possible.

We lead from a position of influence, but we manage from a

position of power. The leader receives his power from the people he leads; the manager receives his power by virtue of his position.

To be a leader you must have people willing to follow you. However, as many have experienced firsthand, it is possible to manage people because of the power of the position whether they want to follow the manager's leadership or not.

THE NEED FOR BALANCE

During the last half of this century there has been a strong emphasis in organizations on management training. Much time, money, and energy has been spent teaching managers how to more effectively manage. Managers in this country have become better planners and organizers. They have mastered the art of cutting costs and increasing profits. They have been taught how to properly evaluate performance and set performance standards. Managers have learned how to utilize and manipulate communication and information systems. They have mastered the art of selling their ideas to others, and they have learned when and how to "close" the deal. And yet, very few managers have been taught the importance of developing strong leadership skills.

Good management skills are a must. You must have them to survive in the highly competitive management profession. However, management skills alone will not help you reach your full potential. You can get by on good management skills at the first-line supervisory and middle-management levels, but you will have to acquire strong leadership skills to continue up the organizational ladder.

Jack Dillard never got his promotion into top management. It wasn't because he didn't know how to manage. He had a proven track record of getting the job done. However, Jack didn't know how to lead people. The further up the organizational ladder you climb, the more essential leadership skills become.

Focus on developing your leadership skills as well as management skills. There are multitudes of good managers, but only a few are also effective leaders. The person with both management and leadership ability is destined to reach his or her full potential in the work world.

DEFINING LEADERSHIP

In *Management: A Biblical Approach* (Victor Books, 1983), I defined management as "meeting the needs of people as they work at accomplishing their jobs" (p. 13). In *The New Leader* (Victor Books, 1987), I said a leader is one who "recruits people to follow his example and guides them along the way while he is training them to do what he does" (p. 16).

According to this definition, the leader is able to recruit people to his or her cause, sets a positive example for people to follow, points the way for people, and works at training people to become leaders.

Leadership skills are more complex than management ones. Management skills deal with the various tasks and functions people perform, such as planning, decision-making, and time managing. However, leadership involves creating the right emotional climate so that people will be motivated to do the jobs determined necessary by the manager.

Leadership deals more with the processes involved in motivating people, while management concerns itself more with the processes involved in the mobilization of people. Leadership focuses more on the creation of the right attitudes while management is concerned more with making sure the right actions occur, regardless of attitude.

However, industrial psychologists have been telling us for years that right actions are much more likely to occur if the people involved have the right attitudes. Therefore, leadership plays an extremely important role in determining the final outcome of any goal, plan, or activity.

The art of leadership is much more sophisticated than the science of management, because in leadership you are dealing more with human feelings and emotions. It is one thing to know how to develop a good plan, but entirely another to be able to motivate people to achieve the plan. That is where leadership comes in. The planning process is a function of management. However, the motivation of people is a function of leadership. Obviously, any plan becomes worthless unless people become motivated to accomplish it.

INFLUENCE VS. POWER

It is not necessary to have a title or official position to be a good leader. In fact, some of the best leaders are frequently found far from the positions of upper management.

People may follow the manager because they are under the manager's authority. However, that does not mean they are willingly following that person. And unless people are willingly following you, you are not a leader. People follow the leader because they want to, not because they have to. The good manager never uses the power of position to try to lead people, but instead, earns the right to be the leader.

By having the position of manager, a person earns the right to manage. However, having the right to manage does not carry an automatic guarantee of leadership. Your position as manager gives you the right and power to manage, but it does not insure your ability to lead. You must earn the right to lead.

Always remember: the officials of the organization may have picked you as a manager, but it will be the people with whom you work who pick their leader. Unless you are chosen by the organization to manage, and appointed by your people as their leader, you will never reach your full management potential.

THE PROFILE OF AN EFFECTIVE LEADER

During management seminars I am frequently asked to describe an effective leader. It has been my experience that all good leaders emphasize similar things. Therefore, it is possible to describe a profile of an effective leader, as follows:
- Honest concern for people and their needs.
- Actively defends the rights of followers.
- Does not show favoritism.
- Helps others succeed.
- Enthusiastic attitude.
- Gives the credit to followers.
- Can be trusted to fulfill promises.
- Does not use position for personal gain.

Honest concern for people and their needs. This is extremely difficult for some managers. The manager who also works at becoming a good leader will occasionally find himself being pulled in two different directions—toward the concerns of those in charge and toward the needs of his followers.

From a pure management perspective, the manager's first obligation is to his superiors within the organization. However, from a true leadership perspective, the manager's first obligation is to those he leads—his followers. And as a result, the manager who is also an effective leader frequently finds himself being pressured on all sides, as figure 8 below illustrates.

Most managers choose to succumb to the cue of superiors at the expense of subordinates' needs. This occurs because managers believe pleasing their superiors is the key to success. That makes the manager an excellent follower, but it does nothing to develop his or her leadership skills.

It is important that we keep things in proper perspective. Remember, this book is about developing your potential as a manager. It is focusing on those issues that help or hinder the progress

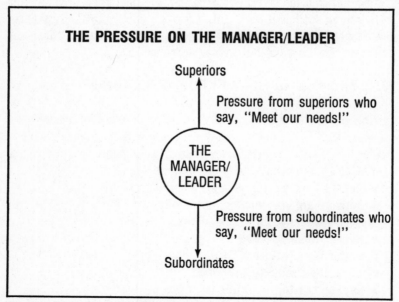

THE PRESSURE ON THE MANAGER/LEADER

Superiors

Pressure from superiors who say, "Meet our needs!"

THE MANAGER/ LEADER

Pressure from subordinates who say, "Meet our needs!"

Subordinates

Figure 8: Illustrates how the manager/leader is frequently caught in the middle between the needs and demands of superiors and subordinates.

of your career. This chapter shows that to develop your full managerial potential you must also become an effective leader.

That means you must develop an honest concern for your people and their needs. Jack Dillard developed an honest concern for what he perceived the needs of his superiors were, and he worked hard to meet those needs. However, meeting the needs of superiors is only half of the job. To become an effective leader you must work equally hard at meeting the needs of your subordinates. You must care as much about those following you as you do about those whom you follow.

The goal is to please both superiors and subordinates. However, there will be times when you are caught in the middle between the two. This is when real leadership skills are important. Your job is to bring the two sides together and arrive at a solution acceptable to both. You must show equal concern for both sides. When you have learned to focus on both the needs of your superiors as well as those of your subordinates, you are well on your way to becoming an effective manager/leader.

Actively defends the rights of followers. The effective leader not only has an honest concern for his followers and their needs, he actively defends their rights as well. For example, while Nehemiah was managing the project of restoring the walls of Jerusalem, the people began to complain that the wealthy Jews in the city were taking advantage of the poor. The poor people were having to mortgage their fields and in some cases even sell their children to have food to eat.

Notice that this problem was not directly related to the management activities associated with building the wall. But Nehemiah got directly involved in the situation and effectively defended the right of those in need. This is the mark of a true leader.

In his role as a leader, the manager may frequently find himself forced to defend the rights of his followers. If you are going to be a leader, you must also be prepared to stand up for the rights of your followers. You must be willing to become an advocate, representing your subordinates' cause to your superiors.

Never be afraid to confront your superiors with the needs of your subordinates. Be polite but firm in your defense of their needs, ideas, and concerns. It is far better to make the needs of your subordinates known to upper management and have those requests refused than to fail to make them known at all. Even if you are unsuccessful in your defense of your subordinates' needs, you will be demonstrating the kind of leadership qualities that will earn you respect. However, in most instances you will find that if you properly justify your subordinates' needs, your superiors will meet those needs.

Wherever you find managers who are weak leaders you will also find a great lack of information moving from that manager's subordinates on up to his superiors. Weak leaders always do a poor job of representing their subordinates to their superiors. On the other hand, strong leaders are quick to defend the rights and present the needs of their followers to their superiors. Therefore, if you want to be an effective leader you must develop a flow of information from your followers to your superiors.

Your followers are looking to you for leadership. They expect you to represent their best interest. At the same time, your superiors are looking to you for leadership, and they expect you to represent their best interest. The effective leader is willing to do both. He becomes the bridge between his followers and superiors that enables effective two-way communication to be developed and maintained. If you aren't willing to do that, you will never experience your full potential as a manager.

As a management consultant, I can assure you that your superiors want to know the needs, concerns, ideas, and opinions of your followers. They not only want to know, they need to know. And that is why they have hired you. They expect you to assume the leadership role of properly representing the needs of both groups. You are the only one who can successfully do that.

Does not show favoritism. The effective leader properly represents both followers and superiors. She maintains objectivity when working with both groups.

One of the worst things you can do as a manager/leader is to favor your superiors at the expense of your followers. Supporting superiors at the neglect of followers may "earn points" and help promote your career for a while, and you may be able to fool your superiors for a period of time. But never forget this fact: *It is the consistent, positive performance and support of your followers*

118

that ultimately proves your ability to manage and lead, and puts you in good standing with your superiors.

You have been hired to effectively manage and lead your followers. Your success as a manager depends on how well you perform that duty. It is extremely important that you properly and fairly lead your subordinates. If you show favoritism either among your subordinates or with your superiors, you will be undermining the trust relationship between you and your followers. Once a group of followers begins mistrusting their leader they no longer recognize that person as their rightful guide and they withdraw their support.

It was not by accident that Nehemiah and his followers rebuilt the wall of Jerusalem in fifty-two days. Much of the credit goes to Nehemiah for his superb management and leadership ability. When Nehemiah discovered that the wealthy Jews in the city were taking advantage of the poor, he confronted the issue. He defended the rights of the poor and confronted the wealthy with their wrongdoing.

If you are interested in developing your full potential as a manager, avoid showing favoritism. Treat everyone justly and fairly. Demonstrate to all concerned, both follower and those you follow, that you are a capable manager/leader deserving their trust.

Helps others succeed. The success of the followers brings success to the leader. In fact, the leader's success is in direct proportion to the success of his or her followers.

Nehemiah was recognized as a great manager and leader, not because of what he did, but because of what his followers accomplished. It was the followers' rebuilding of the wall that earned Nehemiah the reputation of being an outstanding manager.

Nehemiah played an important part in the overall achievement of the goal. However, in the final analysis, it was the actual work and accomplishments of the followers that brought success and recognition to Nehemiah. For without the accomplishments and success of his followers, Nehemiah could have accomplished nothing. And without the accomplishments and success of your followers you will accomplish nothing.

Enthusiastic attitude. The good leader has to have more than just a positive attitude; he must be enthusiastic and inspired. The good leader is enthusiastic about the goal he and his followers are working toward achieving.

Enthusiasm comes from seeing the value of the goal and then making a commitment to achieving it. Steve Brooks, the senior pastor of Springs Community Church in Colorado Springs, says, "Purpose gives direction, and direction produces inspiration and enthusiasm which in turn motivate us to actions that eventually provide us with the satisfaction of a job well done."

That statement is worth remembering. Enthusiasm and inspiration are derived from having a meaningful purpose and direction. It is enthusiasm that helps propel us into actions that lead to success.

If you can't be enthusiastic about what you are doing as a leader, then you should seriously question your role. If you aren't excited about what you are doing, your lethargy will infect your followers.

However, enthusiasm is contagious. For example, Paul, talking to the church in Achaia about the believers in Macedonia, said, "Your enthusiasm has stirred most of them to action" (2 Cor. 9:2, NIV). Enthusiasm is important because it stirs people to action. The enthusiasm of the Christians in Achaia toward giving resulted in the Macedonian Christians becoming excited about giving also.

Are you enthusiastic about the projects and activities you and your followers are involved with, or do you grumble and complain about having to do them? Do you wholeheartedly support the actions and decisions of upper management (you don't have to always agree with your supervisors to support them), or do you ridicule them and complain about the things they do or don't do? The attitudes you display as the leader will be the same attitudes your followers adopt.

Therefore, it is extremely important that you, the leader, be enthusiastic and positive about the organization and its goals, directions, and activities. That does not mean you always have to agree or that you shouldn't be promoting or working toward changes where needed. But as a leader you have the responsibility to enthusiastically support your superiors, whether you always agree or not. That is the mark of a mature leader.

Gives the credit to followers. Who gets the credit for the things accomplished within your area of responsibility? I was asked by The Burdick Companies to conduct an organizational analysis to identify their management strengths and weaknesses. I interviewed approximately thirty employees from a broad cross section of the organization and was greatly impressed with their positive views of the organization.

I later congratulated Roger Burdick, one of the owners, on the strengths of the organization. He replied, "I don't deserve the credit. We have a great family of people here. They work hard, have good ideas, and are the ones that are responsible for whatever success we have experienced."

Roger Burdick is an excellent leader, not because of what he has accomplished, but because he is able to create an environment in which his followers become motivated to do their best.

The employees are given the credit for the company's success, and they in turn are quick to state that their success is a result of the successful leadership for which they have the privilege of working. Without exception, every employee I interviewed at The Burdick Companies praised their top leaders. Even though they may not have understood why, one of the reasons they had such great respect for their leaders was because of the leadership team's quickness in giving credit to their followers.

Let me ask you again, who gets the credit for the things you accomplished within your area of responsibility, you or your followers? The leaders within The Burdick Companies have effectively demonstrated that it pays to give the credit where it is due, and the followers deserve all the credit because they are the ones who make things happen.

As you openly and honestly give credit to your followers, you will discover that they in turn will praise you for making it possible for them to succeed. And one of the best recommendations a manager or leader can have is the recommendation of those he leads.

Can be trusted to fulfill promises. To become a strong leader you must first develop a strong trust relationship with your followers. Always do what you say you will do. Don't tell your subordinates one thing and your superiors another. Be consistent with both. "Say what you mean, and mean what you say" applies to the person wanting to develop as a manager/leader.

By fulfilling your promises you earn the trust and respect of both your subordinates and superiors. And that is one of the most important steps in the development of your potential.

Does not use position for personal gain. Earlier, I noted that we manage from a position of power and lead from one of influence. However, both the manager and leader have power. Power comes to the manager from his superiors. Power comes to the leader from his subordinates or followers. The followers empower their leader as the head of the group. They collectively give up power and subordinate themselves to their leader, otherwise he or she could not lead them.

The effective leader never uses his power to promote his own personal gain. Instead he uses his power in influence to aid and assist others. Followers give power to the leader to enable him or her to effectively lead them, not to abuse that power by using it for selfish gain.

The more power you are able to handle properly and use to serve your subordinates, the greater your potential as a manager and leader. On the other hand, until you begin learning to use your power for the benefit of your followers, you cannot expect to progress very far. You don't deserve more power until you learn to use what you have to serve the needs of others, because that is what leadership and management is all about—serving others instead of self.

PERSONAL APPLICATION

1. What are some ways leaders and managers sometimes misuse their power? What are the results?
2. In your opinion, how is the manager's power that comes from his superiors different from the leader's power that comes from his followers? Why are both important?
3. Which is easier, to manage from a position of power, or lead from a position of influence? Why?
4. How does the leader acquire the influence needed to lead effectively?
5. According to the definition given in this chapter, are you a better manager or leader?

6. What should you be doing to improve your leadership skills?
7. Review your "Personal Profile of Your Management Traits" as recorded in chapter 6. Which traits would you classify as leadership traits, and which ones as management traits?
8. Do you have leadership traits that need to be strengthened or developed? Which ones? How do you intend to develop them?
9. Review the section in this chapter entitled, "The Profile of an Effective Leader." Which of these are your strongest characteristics? Your weakest? How will you improve in your areas of weakness?

9

THE ART OF MANAGING MANAGERS

I recently had a meeting with the Human Resources manager of a nonprofit organization. As I walked into the manager's office I was greeted by a sign on his desk which read, "Six months ago I couldn't even spell *manager,* and now I are one!" Unfortunately, even though that sign was a joke, in far too many instances it becomes frightfully true.

Few people are properly prepared to assume their first job in management. In fact, most people never develop a plan for becoming a manager, and an even fewer number know how to develop their potential once they begin their careers.

That day as I sat in front of his desk, the manager of Human Resources noticed I was looking at his sign. With a broad grin and a tone of voice that seemed to indicate he was bragging, he said, "That's almost true! A year ago I was starving to death as a schoolteacher. Then one day a friend of mine who works here told me they were looking for someone to start a new department called Human Resources. I didn't know much about how to do the job, and they didn't really know much about the kind of person they needed—so here I am!"

He smiled and I tried to muster a smile in return, but inside I felt sorry for him, the organization and people he supervised, and the employees his office was supposed to be serving. Unfortunately, over the years I have met many such people who were ill-prepared to handle the supervisory positions they had been hired to fill.

However, being ill-prepared to handle a management position isn't as bad as remaining incompetent through the years of your tenure. The old saying, "He doesn't have twenty years of management experience; he only has one year of experience repeated twenty times," is the worst criticism that could be made against any manager. Most of us can think of at least one manager to which that statement applies.

An organization or business is only as strong and successful as the people leading and managing it. Therefore, the progressive organization is continually looking for people with highly developed management skills and abilities.

During the past fifteen years that I have been circling the globe as a management consultant and trainer I have observed that there are unlimited possibilities for the individual willing to pay the price to develop his or her potential. There is always plenty of room at the top for the best. However, before you can reach your full zenith you must first learn the art of managing other managers.

MOVING BEYOND THE BASICS

To be successful as a manager you must first master the basic tools of management: planning, decision-making, communications, time management, budgeting, etc. These tools are just as essential to the manager as a hammer, square, saw, and nails are to the carpenter. The supervisor must master these basic management tools because he or she will use them every day.

However, to develop your full potential as a manager you must go beyond the basics. For example, the level and type of management skill required to effectively serve as a CEO of a large organization is much more complex than the skill needed in a first-line supervisory position.

Yes, the CEO must master, and continually use, the basic management skills. But there are also additional abilities required to continue being an effective manager as one moves up the organizational ladder. In this chapter we will examine some of those abilities.

Most people begin their career in management at the first-line supervisory level. At that point they are just one step removed from the frontline employee doing the work and carrying out management's decisions. Therefore, it is extremely important that the supervisor be familiar with the various duties and functions performed by those he or she is supervising.

The first-line supervisor needs to be a specialist in understanding the role of his department or area of responsibility. He is directly involved in the day-to-day activities that collectively serve to accomplish a very important part of management's overall objectives.

However, in most cases the first-line supervisor has a limited view of the organization, its mission, goals, and objectives. He doesn't see the big picture. And in this position the supervisor may be called on from time to time to do the job as well as supervise those doing it.

As the manager advances in his career, instead of supervising the front-line employee, he will begin supervising other managers. This requires a much greater level of sophistication than the basic management skills.

The individual in middle and upper management must begin looking at the overall picture of the organization. He must plan further in advance and make decisions that impact a much broader area of the organization. Instead of being responsible for just one area or department, the manager will become responsible for many areas, departments, or even divisions. And it will become increasingly necessary for him or her to become more of a generalist than a specialist.

MOVING FROM SPECIALIST TO GENERALIST

Traditionally it has been the "specialist" that has been promoted into supervisory and management positions. The best carpenter is generally offered the job of foreman when an opening occurs. The most skilled and knowledgeable workers on the assembly line are usually the ones promoted first into supervision. The best design engineer is usually the person that moves into a supervisory position.

However, the best specialists do not necessarily make the best managers. In fact, being an expert in an area can hinder the development of one's management potential. People who consider themselves specialists frequently have a hard time "letting go" of those responsibilities when they are promoted. They tend to overemphasize their specialty while neglecting their other duties.

For example, while I was in graduate school I worked part-time as the night supervisor of the quality assurance department of a local manufacturing company. My boss, the production manager of the night shift, had worked in the area of quality assurance while in the military. And when he went to work for the company, he helped write the first quality standards and specifications for the production line.

He had trained every quality control inspector in the company, and he trained me in my job even though we had someone whose job it was to train all the new people in that department. During the night shift he spent most of his time in my department instead of taking care of his other production duties.

He obviously was an expert in quality assurance, but he was not a very good production manager because he was unable to focus in areas outside his speciality.

As a result, he was never able to expand his vision to see that every other department was just as important as the quality assurance department. This greatly limited his effectiveness as he moved up the organizational ladder. He was a very poor production manager because he could never make the transition from a specialist to a generalist.

Become more of a generalist as you move further up the organizational ladder. Develop a general working knowledge of the various departments you oversee and recognize that they are all equally important.

As you move up the organizational ladder your job will focus more on leading and managing specialists than being a specialist yourself. You must take on the role of serving the needs of the specialist so that he or she can more effectively accomplish the job.

YOUR JOB IS TO MAKE OTHERS SUCCESSFUL

While you were a specialist, your job was to be as personally successful as possible. Your success was determined by what you accomplished. However, as you move up the organizational ladder and begin managing other supervisors your role must change. Your success is not determined by what you personally accomplish; it is determined by what you help others accomplish. The art of managing managers involves helping the managers under you become as successful as possible. Your success is determined by their success. This is the point Jesus Christ was teaching His disciples. Let's look at it again: "Jesus called them together and said, 'You know that the rulers of the Gentiles lord it over them, and their high officials exercise authority over them. Not so with you. Instead, whoever wants to become great among you must be your servant, and whoever wants to be first must be your slave" (Matt. 20:25-27, NIV).

There is a very important principle in the passage related to managing managers. Your job is to serve their needs so that they will become successful. As you move up the organizational ladder, it is critical that you effectively serve the managers below you so they can become successful in their roles. Simply put, more is at stake if they are unsuccessful. That is why Jesus said the person at the top becomes the "slave" of those below him. He must pour all of his energies into making his executive team successful because if they fail, he fails. You must never forget that your success is measured by how well you help the managers under you to succeed.

I first met Judy Thornton while conducting a management seminar in Europe. She is a very aggressive, goal-oriented lady who started out in sales with an international corporation and is now the vice president of marketing for the company's European operations.

I spent a considerable amount of time discussing with Judy the various problems women face in a management career and during our conversation she said, "I am a very competitive person. I've had to compete in what has traditionally been considered a man's world. I feel I've had to work harder and do a better job to get the same promotions some of my male peers have gotten."

When I asked her what she considered to be the most difficult aspect of management she said, "Learning to channel my energy and drive to help the managers under me become successful. I have always been very success oriented. I have worked hard in order to accomplish my personal goals in life. And it took me a long time to realize that in order to achieve my goals in management and reach the top I had to focus on helping the managers under me achieve their goals first."

Judy was convinced that she was given the vice president job because she had learned to help those managers under her achieve the goals for their departments.

"There were lots of men in the company who were managing larger marketing departments than mine when this job opened up in Europe," Judy said. "But none of them had a better track record of helping the managers under them achieve their departmental goals than mine. I feel I got the job because I knew how to use the power in a management position to serve the needs of the managers under me. That's how I get results!"

THE ROLE POWER PLAYS IN MANAGING MANAGERS

Your job as a manager of managers is to help your managers succeed. You must use the power of your position to serve the needs of the managers under you. And one of the needs they have is decision-making power. Your managers must have the power to make decisions and take the actions needed to succeed. You must empower them to do their job. Giving them decision-making power is one of the best ways you can serve the managers under you.

The further up the organizational ladder you climb, the more power you control. You should be delegating this power to the managers under you. Use your power to serve the needs of the managers under you.

However, as you rise in the company you have more responsibility to insure that power is used properly. Therefore, you not only give decision-making power, but clearly define the perimeters of the power delegated. In doing so you will be able to delegate large amounts of decision-making power to your managers without losing control of the results.

For example, as figure 9 on page 130 illustrates, it isn't enough to just give your managers the power to hire employees. To insure that the right kinds of employees are hired you must set the boundary lines.

The diagram illustrates that in delegating decision-making power to hire new employees, you must also define the limits of that

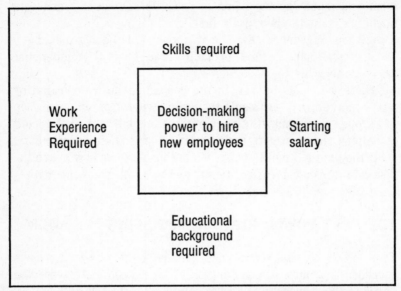

Figure 9: The square represents the decision-making power given to hire employees. The lines of the square illustrate the perimeters concerning how the power is to be used.

power. The manager has the right to hire anyone she chooses as long as they meet the requirements.

It is important that you always negotiate with the person receiving the decision-making power. In other words, if you are giving your manager the power to hire his or her employees, define the boundary lines of that power. By giving your managers boundaries of power you will find them much more effective in the use of it.

DEVELOP A WORK PLAN WITH YOUR MANAGERS

You must learn how to spend quality time with your subordinate managers. This seems like such an obvious point, but very few people in middle- and upper-management positions meet weekly with each individual manager.

During the last fifteen years I have interviewed hundreds of managers in all types of organizations and most, if not all, of those managers have told me they felt a need for more quality personal time with their supervising manager. And of that group, many admitted they felt the time spent with their supervising managers could be much more productive.

Most managers are very busy people. They feel they attend too many meetings that are a waste of time, and as a result, are reluctant to agree to having another meeting unless it is going to meet a need or produce a positive result. Therefore, I am always reluctant to recommend another meeting as a means of solving a problem.

However, I strongly recommend that every manager of managers have a weekly meeting individually with each of his or her managers to develop and evaluate a "personal work plan" as outlined in figure 10 on page 132.

The starting point is to inform your management team of your plans to begin meeting with them to develop and evaluate a "personal work plan." Ask each manager to begin thinking of the goals and objectives they hope to achieve during the next several months and set a time to meet with each manager.

During the first meeting explain that the goal is to agree on specific, measurable work objectives and then determine how you should be serving their needs as they work at accomplishing these. I suggest you prepare a three-ring binder for each of your managers and that you have a three-ring binder on each of your manager's personal work plans.

Bring the binders with you to the first meeting and using the model outlined in figure 10 explain the purpose and process of each weekly meeting. It is important that you get them involved in this process by letting them suggest the objectives they feel should be accomplished. You are there to guide them and make sure the objectives are realistic, meaningful, and accomplishable.

As you agree on the objectives, record them in the upper left-hand section of the page as illustrated in figure 10. Next determine with your subordinate what he or she will need from you to accomplish the objective and record what you will do in serving that work-related need. This information should be recorded in the upper right-hand part of the form as shown in figure 10.

Once this is accomplished, help your subordinate identify any personal development goals he or she should be working on and

MANAGEMENT WORK PLAN

Manager's Name _____ Date _____

YOUR SUBORDINATE'S WORK PLAN	YOUR PERSONAL WORK PLAN
I. Meet with the manager under you and together develop his or her major work objectives to be accomplished over the next several months. Make sure these objectives are measurable by stating exactly what will be accomplished, and by when each objective will be accomplished. II. Also help the subordinate develop a set of personal growth and development objectives.	I. Once you have worked with your subordinate to develop his or her major work objectives, list the things you need to do to effectively serve his or her needs so the objectives may be accomplished as effectively as possible. This becomes your work plan that serves the needs of the subordinate's work plan. Be as specific as possible, stating exactly what, by when, and how much you will do in meeting the work-related needs.
Results of work in progress As you get together each week with your subordinate, evaluate the "work-in-progress" being made on each objective and record the results here. Make notes concerning both positive and negative results, recommendations for improvements, or any modifications of the original objectives.	*Results of work in progress* Each week ask your subordinate to evaluate how well you have done in making progress toward meeting the needs you have committed to meet and record the results here.

Figure 10: The management work plan illustrated above should be used to help set objectives for your subordinates and then evaluate work-in-progress on a weekly basis.

identify what you should be doing to help meet those needs.

Each weekly meeting thereafter you will continue to add any new needed objectives and discuss progress in accomplishing the goals of you and your subordinate. After evaluating the progress, record the results on the appropriate part of the form.

I have used this method for years in my own work and in training hundreds of other managers. It is a very helpful tool for effectively supervising other managers. It also serves as a meaningful evaluative tool.

CONDUCTING MEANINGFUL MANAGEMENT MEETINGS

Meetings are an important part of the process of managing. If you want to become effective, it is imperative that you learn how to conduct meaningful management meetings.

There are basically two kinds of management meetings: information and decision-making meetings. Information meetings are what the name implies; they are designed to impart information, but are not designed to make group decisions. They should be kept as short as possible and called only when necessary.

The bulk of your management meetings should be designed around the purpose of decision-making. Therefore, I will spend the rest of this section explaining the conduct of meaningful management meetings designed around decision-making.

As anyone who has attended many meetings knows, productive meetings don't just happen; they are the result of proper planning and hard work. In fact, in most instances it is the planning done in preparation for the meeting that determines the success and value of the meeting itself.

Therefore, we will begin by looking at the process of planning and preparing for the meeting. Well in advance of the meeting (seven to ten days), send out a partial agenda to those attending and ask for any additions that should be made. Four to five days prior to the meeting send out the actual agenda showing the amount of time allowed for each item on the agenda, as shown in figure 11 below.

When managing managers, one of your jobs involves being the moderator of the management meetings. As moderator, it is your

---

MANAGEMENT MEETING AGENDA DATE *Jan. 8* TIME *8–10 A.M.*

1. Choose a car-leasing plan (presentations by
   George, Linda, and Betty) .... 8:00–8:30 A.M.
2. Review options in new health care plans
   and select the ones best suited to our needs
   (presentation by Frank) .... 8:30–9:15 A.M.
3. Set priorities for space utilization in
   new addition .... 9:15–10:00 A.M.
4. Adjourn at 10:00 A.M. sharp

Figure 11: Sample management meeting agenda showing time allowed for each agenda item.

job to see that the proper items are on the agenda and the proper amount of time allotted to each item. It is also your responsibility to see that the meetings start on time, that the format is adhered to, and that the meeting ends on time. One of the biggest complaints managers voice against meetings is that they drag on too long.

Notice that the agenda shown in figure 11 focuses on decision-making. The moderator's role is to make sure the proper information is presented so the best possible decision can be made. People need to come prepared to make a decision. If at all possible, people should be given copies of presentations prior to the meeting so they can be better prepared for the meeting.

In addition, it is your job to appoint a secretary for the meeting. In most cases the moderator's personal secretary should assume the role since he or she will be dealing with the results of the meeting anyway. If this is not possible, another secretary should serve in that position. Members of the management team should not also serve as secretary. To do so greatly limits their personal input and involvement during the meeting.

In addition to the minutes made by the secretary, the moderator should also record all decisions made and those responsible for carrying them out. This is to help insure that this information is properly recorded and that it becomes a part of the personal work plan of the appropriate individuals as quickly as possible. Once the meeting is over, a summary of the decisions made along with who is responsible for their implementation should be forwarded to all members present and anyone else who needs to know.

YOUR ROLE AS A FACILITATOR

In addition to assuming the role of "moderator" during the meetings, you also need to play the role of a "facilitator." Your job is not to run the meeting, forcing people to buy into your hidden agenda or predetermined decisions. Your role is to draw information, ideas, views, and opinions out of your management team so they can arrive at the best decision possible.

You are there to stimulate, encourage, and help motivate your managers to be innovative in their decisions. Stretch their thinking and encourage them to make the best decisions possible. Your job is to draw out ideas, help develop alternatives, and formulate the actions, plans, and decisions that will allow the managers under you to achieve success. As you do that, you will discover that people look forward to the meetings instead of dreading them.

People often ask me how often management meetings should be held. In most cases it will not be necessary to have a weekly staff meeting once you begin meeting individually with your managers. Your managers will be much more interested in the individual meeting focused on personal work plans than the traditional weekly staff meetings that usually focus on "show-and-tell."

As a general rule of thumb, management meetings probably won't be needed more often than once a month. The important thing to remember is have meetings only when they are needed. Never have meetings just because they are on the schedule.

LET YOUR MANAGERS MANAGE

Contrary to many executive beliefs, moving up in the company does not have to mean that you take on more work. It does mean that you become ultimately accountable for seeing that more work gets done, but that is far different from you doing more work.

Many managers moving up the ladder spend more time on the job and work longer and harder. However, that does not necessarily mean they are better managers or getting more done. In fact, in most instances it means the work isn't getting done by others, and thus the manager has to work overtime.

Let your managers manage. Don't do their jobs for them. Don't let them delegate back up to you the jobs that you have given to them. They have been hired to manage and supervise a department, so let them do it.

I am amazed at how many executives are burdened down trying to do the work they hired their managers to do. The art of supervision involves letting the manager manage. When she has a problem, let her work with her people to solve that problem. Never let a manager bring you a problem unless she also brings you ideas concerning the best ways to solve it.

Every time you solve a problem for your managers, you are not only doing their job for them, but you are cheating them out of the opportunity to grow and develop. You are keeping them from using the creative ideas within their departments to find the solution. And in almost every instance, the solutions generated by those faced with the problems will be far better than those you might offer.

This does not mean you ignore your managers' problems. Their problems, left unsolved, do eventually become your problems. However, your job is not to solve their problems, but to make sure they have the tools to resolve their concerns. Always require them to develop several possible solutions to choose from in their problem-solving process. Then if you are to become involved, it will only be in helping evaluate their possible solutions and giving input from your perspective.

The art of managing managers has nothing to do with how well you solve your managers' problems, but it has everything to do with how well you serve their needs, enabling them to solve their problems for themselves.

PERSONAL APPLICATION

1. If you are already a manager, what additional management skills do you need to acquire, or continue developing, to advance to the next stage in your career?

2. If you are not a manager, what skills should you develop to become qualified to manage others? What will you do to begin developing those skills?
3. As a manager, what should you be doing to help those under you become more successful?
4. If you manage other managers, how can you use the power of your position to better serve the needs of those under you?
5. What are the barriers that keep you from delegating more decision-making power to those under you? What can you do to begin overcoming those barriers?
6. Begin meeting with your supervisors and managers to develop a personal work plan as outlined in figure 10 on page 132. As you do this, keep track of the improvement in your ability to meet the work-related needs of those you manage.
7. What problems do you encounter when conducting management meetings? Could these problems be overcome by implementing the "Conducting Meaningful Management Meetings" section?
8. Apply the principles from "Conducting Meaningful Management Meetings" and evaluate the results. You should find that your meetings are much more productive and beneficial for those involved.

10

TRAINING OTHERS
TO SUCCEED

From a biblical perspective, one of the least understood principles of management is that to succeed as a manager you must first help others be successful. I have said this several times but it bears repeating: *Your job as a manager is to serve the needs of others. Your job is to help others succeed, because you can never be successful as a manager until those under you are first.*

DEVELOP A COACH'S MENTALITY

Excellent coaching is required to produce a winning team. However, coaches, no matter how good they are, never win a single game. It is the players who win. But the players, no matter how skilled, will not win unless properly coached.

The principles in becoming a successful manager are, in many ways, similar to the principles of becoming a successful coach. Both must focus on the following:
- Be committed to success.
- Be competitive.
- Be developing the skills of others.
- Be successful by helping others succeed.

Be committed to success. You must first develop the goal to become the best manager possible before you can ever expect to develop your full management potential. Every professional football coach sets his sights on winning the Super Bowl because that represents being the best. To reach your potential as a manager you must follow that example.

However, many Christians feel it is wrong to want to be the best. They have been taught that the "settle for" mentality is a sign of spiritual maturity and tend to quote the Apostle Paul: "I have learned the secret of being content in any and every situation" (Phil. 4:12, NIV). They justify their lack of motivation to succeed by quoting this passage.

I am not advocating the so-called "prosperity doctrine" which states that God always promises wealth to every Christian, but the Bible is filled with statements that challenge us to allow God to do great things through us. Therefore, I have to believe that God wants us to be committed to being successful at whatever we are doing.

Earlier in the book we looked at Colossians 3:23: "Whatever you do, work at it with all your heart, as working for the Lord, not for men" (NIV). That command includes our careers. You should work "with all your heart" to be as successful a manager as possible, not just to bring glory to yourself, but to bring glory to God.

Be competitive. Our attitude should be like Paul's when he said: "Do you not know that in a race all the runners run, but only one gets the prize? Run in such a way as to get the prize. Everyone who competes in the games goes into strict training. They do it to get a crown that will not last; but we do it to get a crown that will last forever. Therefore I do not run like a man running aimlessly; I do not fight like a man beating the air. No, I beat my body and make it my slave so that after I have preached to others, I myself will not be disqualified for the prize" (1 Cor. 9:24-27, NIV).

Paul is pointing out the importance of a competitive spirit in both our "secular" and "spiritual" lives. Whether we are running a physical or spiritual race, we must run to win. We must prepare ourselves mentally, physically, emotionally, and spiritually in order to win the race of this life.

Be developing the skills of others. The coach must concentrate on developing the skills of his players. He must train them in the fundamentals of the game. If he's coaching football players he must train his players to block, run, pass, and kick the ball. The better job he does at training them in the fundamentals, the better team he will have.

The same is true of the manager. He must teach his people how to be good planners, organizers, leaders, and controllers. The better job he does at training his people in the techniques, the more successful they will eventually become.

Be successful by helping others succeed. One of your primary roles as a manager is to train your people to become successful. Your success depends on how well you play that role. However, helping others become successful becomes very threatening for some managers. In fact, one of the main reasons many managers are reluctant to help their people succeed is because they selfishly want credit for any achievement.

King Saul, Israel's first king, is a classic example of such a leader. The story unfolds in 1 Samuel 17–18. Israel was going to war with the Philistine army. The two armies are lined up on two hills facing each other, and Goliath, the Philistines' mightiest warrior, issued a challenge for Israel to send one of their men to fight him, with the victor's army being the winner of the battle.

All of the Israelites, including Saul their king, were afraid of Goliath. Saul, who stood head and shoulders above all the other soldiers in Israel, was the logical one to fight the giant, Goliath, but even he refused.

Saul became so desperate to find someone to fight Goliath that he offered a large amount of money, his daughter in marriage, and the exemption of all taxes for the father's family of the Israelite soldier who would go fight Goliath. At this point in the story it appeared that King Saul wished to bestow great honor and recognition on the person who would fight this giant. Saul was desperate to find a worthy warrior.

However, after young David, the sheepherder, successfully fought and killed Goliath, King Saul could not handle one of his subjects receiving more credit than himself. Instead of giving David the promised rewards, the next day Saul set out on a campaign to try to kill the young man.

Saul's reaction is similar to the jealous reaction many managers have to the success of their subordinates. Such jealousy will also prove disastrous for any manager.

Saul failed to recognize that the success of his warriors created his success in battle. For Saul to succeed his fighting men had to succeed. However, when they succeeded, Saul wanted the recognition they rightfully deserved. His unwillingness to give them credit helped lead to his downfall as king of Israel.

TRAINING VS. MANAGING

One of your primary roles is to train those under you to become successful. Your success as a manager depends, for the most part, on how well you fulfill that role. Therefore, *it isn't just your ability to manage, but your ability to train others to manage that determines your potential.*

Donald Lopez is an excellent example of that principle in action. I first met Donald several years ago while having lunch at his Mexican restaurant. At that time Donald was the cook, his wife and daughter were the waitresses, and his son was the busboy.

Donald served excellent Mexican food and I soon became a regular customer. While I was eating at Donald's place one evening, he struck up a conversation and I learned that he had big plans for the future. His goal was to develop the best Mexican restaurant in the state.

Later as his restaurant grew, Donald explained to me, "I have an opportunity to take over a Mexican food restaurant that went broke, but I'm discovering I don't have the people trained to start managing another restaurant, and I'm too busy here to try to do it all myself."

I realized that Donald Lopez had fallen into the same trap lots of businesspeople get caught in. He knew what it took to develop a highly successful business, but he didn't know how to train other people to manage.

I began to work with Donald, showing him the importance of becoming a good trainer as well as a good manager. He spent time with his key employees teaching them the tricks of the management trade.

A couple of years ago Donald opened a second restaurant. Last month he opened his third restaurant on the other side of the state. Recently I had lunch with Donald again and he said, "The day you told me I needed to be just as concerned about training my people as I was about doing a good job of managing, you helped change my life forever. As long as you are content just to do a good job as a manager, you can never build an organization bigger than your own ability to manage. But when you begin training others under you, there is no limit to what can be accomplished!"

PREPARING YOUR PEOPLE TO BECOME MANAGERS

I learned a long time ago that just because a person was a good manager didn't mean he knew how to train others. Therefore, in this section we will look at the step-by-step process involved in training people to become effective managers.

STEP ONE: Emphasize the importance of learning to follow instructions. Learn how to give instructions that can be easily followed. People can't follow instructions they can't understand Take the time to make sure people understand your instructions. A person can never be a good leader until he first learns to become a good follower.

Managers frequently fail to give instructions that can be quickly and easily understood by their subordinates. There are many reasons why that happens. The manager is usually busy and not able to take the time to properly explain what he or she wants. The manager may assume that people know what to do; therefore, he doesn't see the need to explain the instructions. Or the manager may know how to do the job so well that he naturally assumes others do also.

Never assume people know what you want done or how you want it done. Always make sure you give clear instructions. If it is a complex job, break it down into easily-digested segments.

Once you do this, begin evaluating your people on how well they follow instructions. Let it be known that those employees who learn to follow instructions will be given the greater opportunity for advancement. Encourage people to ask questions if they don't understand what is expected. Emphasize the point that there is no such thing as a "dumb" question.

STEP TWO: Ask people for input on improving what is being done. Again, this seems like such a simple point, yet it is very important in developing people. Asking for input accomplishes several things.

First, it forces people to begin thinking seriously about their job—why they do what they do and how it could be improved. It stimulates creativity and communicates to employees that their ideas are important.

Second, it provides the manager with the opportunity to evaluate the employee's ability to do creative thinking and to understand the fundamentals of the job.

Third, it means the manager must be willing to use those good ideas and suggestions that are offered by the employees.

Once you begin asking for input and discover an employee able to offer meaningful suggestions, you are ready to take him or her to the next step of development.

STEP THREE: Assign the employee the task of planning and carrying out a special project with input from you. This is an important step in training your people to be managers. As the manager, you will first have to develop a special project for the employee to work on. This may be a project the employees would be working on anyway, or you may have to create a specific project for the employee. Either way, it will be necessary for you to give the employee the following instructions:

1. The employee is to develop the plans for how the project or assignment will be completed.
2. The employee will develop measurable objectives for the project.
3. Once steps 1 and 2 are completed the employee will meet with you, the manager, to review those plans and objectives. You will provide input as needed and evaluate with the employee's ability to set measurable goals and objectives.
4. The employee will then determine the resources needed in terms of materials, equipment, people, time, and money required to accomplish the project.
5. The employee will then meet with you to review his "budget" for the project and you will evaluate how well he has done and give any input as needed.
6. During this entire process (steps 1–5) you will also evaluate how well the employee takes suggestions from you and how he or she handles constructive criticism.
7. You are now ready to let the employee begin carrying out this special project. As he does so you will have to meet with him or her periodically to evaluate work-in-progress and offer input.
8. Once the project is completed you will have to meet with the employee to evaluate not only the success of the job itself,

but how well the employee did in applying such management skills as planning, organizing, leading, and controlling.

Once you are satisfied that the employee is able to handle planning and organizing functions effectively, you are ready to move on to the next stage in his or her managerial development.

STEP FOUR: The employee designs and carries out a project that involves leading and supervising the work of others (with input from you). In this step you repeat points 1–8; however, you add the responsibility of supervising others as part of the project. During this step you will need to pay special attention to how well the employee is able to work with those he is leading, how effective he is at communicating with others, and how well he serves the needs of those he leads.

You will also need to evaluate how open the employee is to accepting ideas from others working under his direction and if he is able to effectively deal with conflicts that may arise.

During this step you have two objectives. One, you want the employee to continue developing his management skills. However, you also want to be developing the employee's leadership skills. The employee must begin learning how to effectively serve the needs of others as they work at accomplishing their jobs. He must learn how to evaluate their work and provide proper recognition, both constructive criticism as well as verbal praise.

STEP FIVE: Continue assigning larger projects with greater responsibility for planning, organizing, leading, and controlling to improve managerial proficiency. People learn to manage by managing. You must create situations that allow them to manage. Your objective is to gradually give them greater responsibility.

For example, I recently conducted a management training program for a group of managers in Europe. During one of the breaks in our meeting a manager told me, "I can see I need to begin involving my supervisors under me in the process of hiring people to work in their departments."

The manager had been hiring all the employees that worked under his various supervisors. As a result, some of his supervisors were complaining about the quality of people they were getting. He recognized that by teaching them how to do the interviewing, he would have more time to do the things he should be doing.

For that manager, it was a step in the right direction. He was learning that his role was to develop ways to get his supervisors directly involved in doing the things that he had been doing for them. That is the way you develop managers. You involve people in doing the things you usually do as a manager.

STEP SIX: Begin working on an opportunity for the employee to supervise his or her own area. Your job is not completed until you have helped the employee become a supervisor. At that point you are ready to assume a new role with the employee—the role of "mentor."

ASSUMING THE ROLE OF MENTOR

The six steps listed above are designed to prepare your employees to begin a career in supervision and management. They lay the foundation for preparing a person to *begin* a career in management. They, by themselves, do not make a person a good manager.

Once you take a person through the six steps listed above and assign him to a supervisory or entry management position, you are ready to assume the role of "mentor." The dictionary describes a mentor as a *wise, loyal advisor.*

Very few managers ever learn to assume the role of mentor to those emerging managers under them. Until you become a mentor to another developing manager you have missed one of the most rewarding experiences in management. Most people are reluctant to be a mentor because they have never had the privilege of having one. However, I have never met a person in management who didn't wish for someone to take them under his or her wing and help them learn.

As a mentor you become an example for your managers to follow. We see this pattern in the Apostle Paul's life: "Follow my example, as I follow the example of Christ" (1 Cor. 11:1, NIV), and "Join with others in following my example, brothers, and take note of those who live according to the pattern we gave you" (Phil. 3:17, NIV). Paul was a firm believer in the value of mentoring. He was willing to become the example for others to follow.

As a mentor to your developing supervisors, you must be willing to pass on to others the things you have learned. You must communicate your willingness to teach and train your people from your own experiences. And you must be willing to be open and honest concerning your own strengths and weaknesses. Teach what you know, but never be afraid to say, "I don't know, but I will find out the answer for you."

As a mentor focus on the following:

- Pass on your vision and purpose.
- Work on teaching principles, not a list of "do's" and "don'ts."
- Emphasize the importance of values.
- Teach your people how to grow through their failures.
- Keep emphasizing the basics.
- Challenge them to be all they can be.

Pass on your vision and purpose. It isn't enough to just teach people the fundamentals of management; we must also help them develop a vision for life.

For example, generations of the Wiseman family spent their lives working in the coal mines in Kentucky. They were simple people and lived a simple life.

Herbert Wiseman was born in 1910 and at an early age joined his father, brothers, and uncles working in the mines. But Herbert was different from the rest of his family. He wasn't content to live out his life in the mines as generations of his family had done before him.

He wanted to see the world and all the things the world had to offer. At the age of sixteen he packed a few things in a flour sack, caught a freight train headed west, and set out to see the world beyond the Kentucky horizon. He worked for a while as a dishwasher in a Denver hotel, and then headed west to California.

He got another job in a hotel, this time as a night clerk. Over the next few years Herbert learned the hotel business as he slowly worked his way from job to job up through the organization. It was in California that Herbert developed his dream of owning hotels all over the world.

He worked hard, saving every penny except for what he absolutely had to spend to exist. When he wasn't working at the hotel he worked nights at a variety of odd jobs. And during the Depression while other people were having a hard time making ends meet, Herbert was able to continue to save money.

At the end of the Depression Herbert Wiseman bought his first hotel in Los Angeles. It was a very small, run-down building in one of the poorest parts of town, but Herbert was on his way to living his dream. He worked hard cleaning, painting, and remodeling the building, doing most of the work himself.

Two years later he sold the hotel for a nice profit and invested in a larger hotel and some vacant land nearby. Over the next four decades Herbert Wiseman built a financial empire in real estate, mining operations, and banking. He owned investments in many countries of the world and lived his dream.

Herbert Wiseman died in Singapore in 1986 while vacationing at one of the many homes he owned throughout the world. He left behind a son and daughter, three grandchildren, and hundreds of millions of dollars in investments.

I met his son, Robert, while speaking at a Christian businessmen's luncheon and later did some consulting work for him. One evening while I was visiting Robert and his wife, Jennifer, in their home, Robert said, "Myron, my father was a great self-made man. He went from rags to riches just like the stories in the movies. He was a fine Christian and a good father. He left us a financial empire, but he never passed on his dream."

I spent the rest of the evening listening to Robert vent his frustrations with his life. He had more money than he could spend in a lifetime. He had a beautiful wife and family and was well respected in both business and Christian circles, but he was a very unhappy man.

"I really resent my father," he said. "Dad had a dream he worked for all his life, but he never shared it with me. And now I have what his dream produced, but I don't have his dream."

One of your major roles as a mentor is to pass on the dream. You can teach people to be excellent managers, help them acquire great financial possessions, but if you don't help them develop vision, life will have very little meaning.

Challenge your managers with developing a purpose for their lives. Share your own and explain how it has helped you. It is your vision that gives meaning to your management. Pass it on.

Work on teaching principles, not a list of "do's" and "don'ts." By emphasizing the principles of management you force your subordinates to think for themselves; whereas, when you give them a list of do's and don'ts you do the thinking for them.

For example, you don't teach the importance of performance evaluations by simply reviewing a set of forms used to measure and evaluate performance. You teach the need and importance of performance evaluations by discussing the principles involved. You don't teach time management by simply handing a manager a "pocket calendar"; you must present the principles of time management. But until the manager understands the principles involved, why they are important, and what they will do for him, he probably won't be very interested in using the tools.

Emphasize the importance of values. Your role as mentor is very different from that of the classroom teacher. You are working with your people on a daily basis. You not only teach by what you say, but more importantly, you teach by example.

You are teaching by your example whether you intend to or not. Your people listen to what you say, but what you do has a much greater impact on them. And your value system plays a major role in determining what you do.

If your value system says, "Go ahead and do it, just don't get caught," then you will act that way. You may say it is wrong to cheat and steal, but if you falsify expense account records you are really communicating the opposite value.

One of your major roles as a mentor is to help develop within your people strong convictions concerning values. The Ten Commandments exemplify the core biblical values that a Christian businessperson should follow.

Teach your people how to grow through their failures. You and your people will fail from time to time, but always remember: *how you deal with failure is much more critical than the failure itself.*

Most of us have been taught to believe that failure is bad and should be avoided at all costs. It is true that failure can be very bad; however, it doesn't have to be a negative, it can become a positive. For example, notice what James 1:2-4 tells us. "Dear brothers, is your life full of difficulties and temptations? Then be happy, for when the way is rough, your patience has a chance to grow. So let it grow, and don't try to squirm out of your problems.

For when your patience is finally in full bloom, then you will be ready for anything, strong in character, full, and complete" (TLB).

Problems and failures can work to our advantage if we are willing to learn from them. Thus, instead of seeing failure strictly as negative we must view it as an opportunity to learn, grow, and develop.

The worst thing about failure is what it does to our attitudes. Failure tends to create negative feelings, reactions, and atmospheres. Your job as a mentor is to communicate that you want to avoid failures, but when they occur you will work with those involved to turn them into positive learning experiences.

When there is a failure, approach it from the perspective of "we failed" instead of "you failed." In all probability you somehow contributed to that failure. Remember that your job is to serve the needs of your people. Therefore, when they fail, it probably is the result of some type of unmet need. Maybe they needed more training, equipment, time, help, or information. If there was an unmet need that caused the failure then you contributed to that failure.

That is why you should always approach a failure from the standpoint of "we failed." Begin your investigation by asking how you could have better served their needs to prevent the failure. Then explore what caused the failure and what needs to happen to turn the situation around.

Keep emphasizing the basics. No matter where you and your subordinates are on the organizational ladder you need to emphasize the basic management functions of planning, organizing, leading, and controlling. Continually work with your people in the development and improvement of these basic management skills. Evaluate your people's basic performances regularly and make them a major part of your focus as a mentor.

Challenge them to be all they can be. To reach your management potential you must not only be effective at managing material resources, you must also become effective at developing your human resources. In fact, it is the effective management of human resources that determines the ultimate potential of any manager, business, or organization.

As a mentor, your goal isn't just to reproduce yourself as a manager, it is to help those under you develop their full potential. Hopefully, with your help your people will be able to achieve even greater things than you are currently achieving.

Notice what Jesus told His disciples. "I tell you the truth, anyone who has faith in Me will do what I have been doing. He will do even greater things than these, because I am going to the Father" (John 14:12, NIV). Jesus Christ's goal was for His disciples to do even greater things than He had done. And that must be the goal of every mentor.

The goal isn't just to bring your people up to your level; it is to help them learn from you and incorporate that with what they already know so they may go on to achieve greater things. *Managing to Be the Best* involves helping your people become all they can be, and anything less is only second best.

PERSONAL APPLICATION

1. Has your view of your role as a manager changed as a result of reading this chapter? If so, how?
2. Review the section entitled, "Develop a Coach's Mentality."
   a. As a manager works to develop his people's management skills, why is it important for him to assume the role of a coach?
   b. What is the difference between the coach and the player?
   c. What contribution does the coach make in the success of the team?
   d. How does that apply to your role as a manager?
   e. What should you be doing to improve your coaching skills?
3. Why is it important for the manager to also become an effective trainer?
4. Why don't more managers see their role as trainers also?
5. Are there things you need to work on to become a more effective trainer? If so, what?
6. Develop an action plan for training your people to become more effective and productive supervisors.
7. Review the section, "Assuming the Role of Mentor."
   a. Did you have a mentor as you developed your management career? If so, what did that person do to help you?

b. What is the difference between a trainer and a mentor?
8. What is your dream or vision for life and how is that being accomplished through your management career?
9. What are you doing to help your people develop their dreams?
10. What will you do to help your people establish a value system in line with those principles presented in the Ten Commandments?
11. How will you use the principles in this chapter to better develop your management and leadership skills?

11

KEEPING YOUR
LIFE IN BALANCE

I was raised in a very poor community in Oklahoma. But my eighth Christmas taught me just how poor my family was. That realization set the course of my life. My aunt and uncle had just moved into a new home in Oklahoma City, and they invited us to come and celebrate the Christmas holidays with them. I will never forget that experience as long as I live because it was my first trip to the big city and into a world I hadn't known existed.

My eyes must have been as big as saucers as we drove up in front of my aunt and uncle's new brick home. And when we went in their house I got the shock of my life. They had a bathroom in their house! In fact, they had a bathroom on every floor in their house. And they had running water and lights that came on when you flipped a switch.

I was speechless. I walked all through their house just staring at all the beautiful things. We had none of them in our home. I went into the kitchen and turned the faucets and watched the water run down into the sink. I opened the cupboard door under the sink, curious as to where the water was going. I was even more amazed to discover that hot water came out of one of the faucets.

As I grew up I determined that someday I would make lots of money so I could live like my aunt and uncle in the city. I dreamed of someday owning my own business like my uncle, living in a fine new home, driving a new car, and having all the things that successful people have.

That goal became the driving force in my life. I went to college and on to graduate school. After graduate school I got my first really good job. I was on the way in pursuit of my goal. I began climbing the management ladder and eventually became vice president of administrative services for a manufacturing company. But I had always dreamed of owning my own business, so I resigned and started my own management consulting firm. A few years later a friend and I started a manufacturing company, and then we teamed up with another friend to start a marketing company to market the products we manufactured.

At that point I had three businesses: a management consulting organization, a manufacturing firm, and a marketing company. I bought a new home, one much bigger and nicer than the one my aunt and uncle had in Oklahoma City. I had new cars (two in one year). And I felt I was well on the way to accomplishing the goal I had set for myself as an eight-year-old boy.

I also had become a Christian. I had accepted Christ while in graduate school, and my wife and I were committed to having a "Christian home." I was very active in my church, and was involved in leading home Bible studies with people in our community.

I became busier and busier, both with my career and with my church activities. People began telling me I needed to slow down, but I was having s much fun accomplishing the goals I had set I saw no need to heed their advice.

However, the busier I got with my career and Christian activities the less time I spent with my family. I met their financial needs, but they needed much more than that. They needed me, but I was so busy I didn't have time to give them me. One day my world came crashing down around me (see *Burnout*, Victor Books, 1987). My wife filed for a divorce, and as a result I lost part of my business holdings and most of my credibility in the Christian community.

I became angry at God and the world. A thousand times I asked, "How could this have happened to *me?*" It took the help of one of my business partners to realize I had brought the problems on myself. My life had gotten totally out of balance. I had accomplished my goals, but had forgotten how to really live life.

That happened several years ago and since that event I have discovered multitudes of managers and executives around the world caught in the same trap. Their lives are out of balance, and they too are headed toward disaster in their personal lives unless they learn how to balance their careers with the rest of life.

THE ACTIVITY TRAP

In 1 Kings 20:39-40 there is a short story that teaches a very important management principle. A master told his servant to watch a prisoner. When the master came back to get his prisoner the servant said, "While your servant was busy here and there, the man disappeared" (v. 40, NIV).

Notice that the servant was busy working for the master. He wasn't over under the shade tree taking a nap. He was busy. He was doing all the things that needed to be done for his master, but in his busyness the important job of watching the prisoner didn't get done.

There is a very important lesson for us in this short story. Like this servant, it is easy for us to get caught in the "activity trap." We can become so busy doing things that need to be done, the most important things are left behind.

There is always more work to be done in a day than you can get done, so you start coming in earlier and staying later to "stay on top of things." (I remember doing that for years. In fact, I went eight years without taking a vacation because I was too busy to take the time away from the business.) Then as you get more responsibility you are tempted to start taking work home with you at night. You start skipping lunch, or grab a bite on the run.

Your mind and energies become consumed with your work and the important things you are doing, or maybe not getting done. Instead of you being in control of your job and career, it slowly takes control of you. You are usually late for the evening meal, so your wife and family wind up eating alone—again and again. The evenings you are home your mind is preoccupied with work, and your family is alone anyway even though your body is present.

If the above three paragraphs describe you, then I have some sobering news—your life is out of balance. And I can tell you from experience that a life out of balance is a life on a collision course with disaster.

This is one of the most important chapters in the book because developing and maintaining balance in life is not only important in the development of your management potential, but it is critical to maintaining your success once you reach your career goals. It is one thing to reach the top, but another to remain there. Many a successful executive has fallen simply because he didn't learn how to maintain balance in his life.

Getting caught in the activity trap is one of the major factors leading to life out of balance. Most successful managers and executives are very goal oriented. They have learned how to set goals and accomplish them. They are usually conscientious and hard workers. They have "worked" their way up the ladder. Hard work had paid great dividends for them.

Over the years it becomes easier and easier for them to focus on work, because it is work that has produced their success. That is why so many managers are workaholics.

I became such a person. I was busily involved in the activities and work that I felt was making me successful. However, the more I focused on work, the more my life got out of balance. I slowly forgot how to live and enjoy life. I forgot how to play. For me the journey was no longer as important as the destination.

REAL VS. IMAGINED PRIORITIES

Certainly most, if not all, managers and executives would tell you that their families are more important than their jobs; however, if you were to talk to their families, many would say otherwise.

There are two kinds of priorities—real and imagined—and on the surface it is hard to tell them apart. We give lip service to both kinds of priorities. In most cases we don't even know there is a difference between the two. We talk about imagined priorities as if they were real. In fact, we even say they are real, even though they are imaginary.

For years I said that God was first in my life, my family second, and my business third. I believed that was the actual order of priority. However, it wasn't true. I would have argued with you that it was true, but it wasn't true. That was an imagined order of priority. And I know that now.

The difference between real and imagined priorities is that we always give our time to real priorities. Therefore, if you want to know what is most important in your life look at how you spend your time.

I would never have admitted that making money was more important than my family, but it was true. I imagined that my family was far more important than my businesses, but it was just an imagined priority. My business was far more important to me than my family. I spent almost all of my time, energy, and effort in my career.

Peter Ward, the founder and owner of P.J. Ward and Associates in Toronto, Canada, has taught me valuable lessons in taking time for your family. He recently told me, "It has taken me twenty years to begin learning to *really* put my wife's needs ahead of my business. I would always tell myself the things on my list were much more important than the things on her list, so I always did my list first. The problem was I had so many things on my list, the things she wanted me to do never got done," Peter said.

He went on to explain that he recently realized that he had actually been putting his wife's needs at the bottom of his priority list. "However, I'm working at changing that," he said. "I now try to do the things that she needs done first, and then take care of my own 'do list' for the day. I have discovered that by doing the things she needs done first, I still have all the time I need to get the important things done at work. And putting her needs first has greatly improved our relationship."

Peter Ward has learned that his real priorities are those to which he gives his time. He has made time in his very busy schedule for his wife and family because they are important to him.

If you want to *Manage to Be the Best,* you must begin sorting out your real and imagined priorities. How much time are you giving to your work, family, God, and yourself? The answer to that question will tell you the real order of your priorities.

To reach the top and then manage to stay there, you must develop balance in your life. You can't spend all your time on the job without the rest of your life suffering. Like Peter Ward, you must learn to make time for your family.

I am always amazed at the number of managers who do a good job of planning, delegating, communicating, and managing time on the job, but who are lousy at applying these same important principles in their private lives. And that speaks loud and clear concerning the real priorities in their lives.

FACTORS CONTRIBUTING TO AN UNBALANCED LIFE

There are many factors that cause our lives to get out of balance; however, some of the major ones affecting the manager are listed below:

- Pressure to succeed.
- Competition for positions on the organizational ladder.
- Our concept of "commitment to the company."
- Problems at home.

Pressure to succeed. The pressure to succeed contributes greatly to supervisors' and managers' lives getting out of balance. There is a lot more pressure to succeed on managers than on non-managers because the manager is responsible for a greater part of the overall organization than the single employee doing a specific job or task.

Debbie Collins learned the hard way. She spent two years working on the assembly line for an electronics manufacturing company and then was promoted into a supervisory job. By the time I met her, she had worked her way up the ladder to manager of the production scheduling department.

One day during a lunch break Debbie told me her story. "In some ways I was happier when I was working on the assembly line than I have been since getting into management. There is a lot more pressure to produce now that I am a member of the management team."

Debbie explained that shortly after taking her current job she and her husband had split up largely due to her need to spend more time at the office. "My husband just didn't understand the demands of a job like this. If we don't get our schedules out on time entire assembly lines are shut down. That kind of responsibility places great demands on you. A lot of people are counting on me to do my job."

Debbie told me she liked her job, but she missed being able to go home at night and leave it all behind. She said, "When I worked on the assembly line, my responsibility ended when I walked out the door at the end of my shift. But now I feel the pressure all the time. My responsibility to the company doesn't just end when I drive out of the parking lot at night. I carry the burden and pressures of that responsibility with me all the time."

Debbie Collins' statement sums up the feelings of most people in management. There is a constant feeling of responsibility and pressure to succeed that goes with every job in management. Like one of my former bosses used to say, "Pressure is just part of the job when it comes to management."

It is the pressure to perform, produce, and succeed that causes many managers' lives to get out of balance. They carry their jobs home with them, both in their briefcases and in their minds. They feel the pressure to succeed and produce even when on a weekend outing with the family. And the stronger the pressure, the greater the risk of life getting out of balance.

Competition for positions on the organizational ladder. A great deal of emphasis is placed on the importance of "upward mobility" in organizations today. Managers are expected to strive for advancements and a failure to do so is frequently seen as a lack of commitment to the organization.

As a result, there is tremendous pressure on managers in some organizations to be actively working toward promotions. However, the further up the organization you climb, the fewer promotions there are available. This results in a "catch 22" situation for the manager. It causes managers to spend the extra hours at the office, bring home extra work, and spend every Saturday morning at the plant trying to get caught up.

Some managers not only feel the pressure at work to be working for the promotion, but they can feel the pressure from home as well. Some mates tend to push their spouse to work for the promotion because it will mean more money. Pressures such as these can lead directly to lives out of balance.

Our concept of "commitment to the company." Some organizations still actually measure your commitment to the company by how early you arrive and late you stay at the office. One manager told me, "I go to the office every Saturday morning whether there is a need or not, because I learned a long time ago that was one of the surest ways to show your loyalty to the company and get a raise or promotion."

Such thinking is the norm in many of the larger corporations with their "pecking orders" and bureaucratic approach to organizational dynamics. In such organizations it becomes very important that you demonstrate your commitment by coming early, staying late, and showing up each Saturday morning even if it is only to drink a few cups of coffee with your fellow loyal brethren.

Such actions may fool some, but it does nothing toward keeping one's life in balance. In fact, it takes away time which could and should be used in other meaningful areas of your life.

Relationship problems at home. For many managers spending too much time with their career creates problems at home, but for some it is the domestic difficulties that tend to drive them deeper into their careers. For example, I have a close friend who admittedly spends all the time he can at the office so he doesn't have to put up with a bad situation in his homelife.

He has told me he would prefer to spend more time at home if the atmosphere wasn't so hostile. His wife even jokes that the less she sees him the better she likes their marriage. For my friend, and many others in similar situations, it is the problems at home that have driven them to marry their career. The result is a life totally out of balance.

JESUS CHRIST: A ROLE MODEL OF LIFE IN BALANCE

I think most of us would agree that Jesus Christ led a very busy life during the three years of His active ministry here on earth. Everywhere Jesus went people were continually pressing around Him, clamoring for His attention. Mark 6:31-32 gives us insight into Jesus Christ's hectic schedule and how He dealt with it: "Then, because so many people were coming and going that they did not even have a chance to eat, He said to them, 'Come with Me by yourselves to a quiet place and get some rest.' So they went away by themselves in a boat to a solitary place" (NIV).

Notice that there were so many people around Jesus and His disciples that they couldn't even find time to eat. Most managers can readily identify with that scene. However, also notice that Jesus did not allow that situation to continue. He told His disciples to follow Him and He took them to a quiet place of solitude for rest and relaxation.

Even Jesus Christ realized that He needed a break from His

work. On numerous occasions we see Him slipping off by Himself to a quiet place to be alone, relax, and spend time in prayer with His Father. This was one of the ways Jesus kept His balance in life, even during the midst of the pressures of a rigorous schedule.

DEVELOPING AND MAINTAINING A BALANCED LIFE

The further up the management ladder you climb, the harder you will have to work at keeping your life in balance. Without balance in your life your "success" may be short-lived. To develop and maintain balance in your life, you should apply the following points:

- Have goals for every area of your life.
- Take one weekend a year for planning and evaluating your personal goals.
- Work at developing new and different interests.
- Learn to play as hard as you work.
- Focus on the 80/20 principle.

Have goals for every area of your life. Every manager has a set of measurable goals and objectives he is working to accomplish on the job, but very few take the time to develop measurable objectives for their personal lives. This is one of the reasons their lives tend to get out of balance.

On the job the manager has goals that state exactly "what" is to be accomplished, "how much" is to be accomplished, and "by when" it will be accomplished. In management we call this *measurable* goals, because they are always specific.

These kinds of measurable goals help give the manager direction and purpose. However, if he doesn't have measurable goals in his personal life, when he leaves the job he is without direction or purpose. Therefore, he tends to get all of his sense of accomplishment from his work, so that is where he begins putting all his efforts. And the end result is life out of balance.

Setting goals and objectives for each area of your personal life is one of the surest ways of keeping your life in balance. It will give direction for the time you spend with your family. You will find purpose in your leisure time. Ultimately, it will give more meaning to your spiritual life.

However, in setting those goals, make sure they aren't just an extension of your work goals. For example, don't say, "My personal goal is to make more money." That is an extension of your career goals. Your personal time goals should, as much as possible, be totally unrelated to your career goals. For example, you could have a goal of taking one weekend trip per month with your wife or family. Make a goal to learn one new seasonal sport for each season of the year. You could develop one new hobby each year, and so on.

The important thing is that you begin to set specific goals in all areas of your life, including your family, spiritual life, and leisure time. This will give you new interest and purpose in the areas outside your work and help keep your life in balance.

Take one weekend a year for planning and evaluating your personal goals. Just like work, take time to plan and evaluate the rest of your life. I suggest that once a year you (and your spouse if you are married) take a weekend to get away to plan next year's goals and evaluate the progress made on the current goals.

You should plan this weekend in advance and allow nothing to interfere with it. Pick a place out of the area, but close enough so you don't spend all your time in the car driving. It should be a place where you can relax, enjoy the environment, and play as well as work.

I suggest you leave early enough on Friday to reach your destination by dinner. Spend the evening with your spouse relaxing, having dinner, and enjoying each other's company. The next morning (Saturday) spend the time planning next year's goals and evaluating this year's progress. Take the afternoon off to relax and play. Repeat that same schedule for the following day, work in the morning and relax in the afternoon.

Write down all your goals and have a copy for both you and your mate. Make sure the goals are stated in "measurable" terms, telling specifically "what" is to be accomplished in each area, "how much" is to be accomplished, and "by when" it will be accomplished.

I have had some people tell me once a year was not often enough. They prefer taking a weekend for goal-setting every six months. You should go through the process described above and

161

then determine how often it needs to be repeated. However, it should be done *at least* once a year.

If you are married, you will be working on both personal and family goals. All goals pertaining to marriage and family should be developed jointly. These mutual goals must be developed by both husband and wife.

If you have small children, they should be left with either a baby-sitter or a family member. If the children are older, you will need to decide as a family whether or not they go. They certainly will need input into all goals affecting the family.

This goal-setting and evaluating weekend should cover such areas as: family, spiritual, and personal development goals, hobbies, and use of leisure time. You should also assess your purpose in life, career goals, and personal and family value systems. You should develop both short- and long-range goals as needed. Some goals may be accomplished within a month, season, or year. Others may take many years or your entire lifetime.

You will not only be working to set measurable goals, but you will also need to begin formulating a plan for accomplishing those goals. Goals never accomplish themselves. You must determine the steps and actions you will take to achieve them. As you take the necessary actions you will be building balance into your life. A balanced life builds a meaningful, productive life both at work and play, on and off the job.

Work at developing new and different interests. I have met a number of managers and executives that never read anything other than material related to their business. Such people have stopped growing and developing as individuals. As long as we are developing new and different interests we are growing as people, but as soon as we stop expanding our interests we begin to waste away.

Each year develop new and different interests in your life. This is one of the best ways to continue growing and keep balance between your career and personal life. Most managers enjoy a challenge. Just as you need challenges in your job, you need challenges in your personal life. Work at developing different interests. They will offer challenges to help motivate you outside your career.

Learn to play as hard as you work. By the time they reach forty, most managers and executives have forgotten how to play.

They have spent almost two decades learning how to work, and they do that very well, but in the process of learning how to work hard they have forgotten how to play hard. The result is a life out of balance.

All work and no play will lead to disaster someday. You must learn how to play as hard as you work. As I noted earlier, I went eight years without taking a vacation. I had forgotten how to play.

I couldn't even relax and enjoy a weekend outing with my family without calling to check on things at work. And when I did go away for a weekend I always took plenty of work with me. When my family complained about me working all the time, my response was, "I enjoy my work. It's what I like doing." However, the facts were plain; my life was out of balance. All I knew was work, work, work. Yes, I enjoyed it, but that wasn't the point. I didn't enjoy anything else. I had to relearn how to enjoy things in life other than my work.

Save yourself from this trap. Learn how to play as hard as you work. Develop hobbies, sports, and interests that will allow you to play. Play with your wife and family. Make time for your friends and relatives. Play hard. It will help keep balance between your career and the rest of your life.

Focus on the 80/20 principle. The 80/20 principle states that 80 percent of your results come from 20 percent of your effort. That means that the other 80 percent of your effort is only producing 20 percent of your results.

This principle makes the point that there are only a few things we do each day that are really important, because it is those few things that are producing most of our results. This principle seems to be applicable in all of life. In everything we do, there are usually just a few things that produce most of our results. The other busy work and activity really accomplishes very little. To break out of the unproductive activity trap we need to major on the few things that produce success.

As we saw earlier, the activity trap is one of the major contributing factors of life out of balance. Focusing on the 80/20 principle will help us out of the activity trap and provide us with the needed time to accomplish more productive things.

As you have read through this chapter many of you have been

thinking that you don't have time to do all these things. That probably is true for some of you right now. But one of the ways to find time is to focus on the 80/20 principle. Identify those few things that produce and begin eliminating or minimizing the remaining frivolous activities.

Developing balance between your career and private life is one of the best "insurance policies" you can have for staying at the top of your career. Apply the points and principles presented in this chapter. They will not only help you reach the top in your career and remain there, but they will help you reach the top in your personal life as well.

PERSONAL APPLICATION

1. Review the section entitled, "The Activity Trap."
    a. Do you feel you are caught in the activity trap?
    b. If so, how is it affecting balance in your life?
2. Study the section entitled, "Real vs. Imagined Priorities."
    a. Make a list of your priorities.
    b. Determine how much time you are giving to each priority.
    c. What does this tell you about which ones are actually "real" and which ones are "imagined" priorities?
    d. What actions do you need to take in light of this information?
3. Look again at the section, "Factors Contributing to an Unbalanced Life."
    a. Do you see any of these factors affecting your life? If so, which ones?
    b. What will you do to begin removing these factors that keep you from developing and maintaining balance in your life?
4. Read Matthew 6:31-32.
    a. What principles did Jesus apply in this passage to help maintain balance in His disciples' lives?
    b. What lessons do you learn from this passage that should be applied to your life?
5. Study the section, "Developing and Maintaining a Balanced Life."
    a. Plan a weekend getaway to evaluate your life, set goals, and

make plans for your coming year. Follow the format outlined in this section.

b. What will you begin doing to develop new and different interests in your life? How will this help you to maintain balance in your life?

c. Look at the 80/20 principle and apply it to the various aspects of your life. What does it reveal about how you have been spending your time? How will it help you develop more balance in your life?

12

GOD'S PLAN
FOR YOUR CAREER

We have reached the final, and most important, chapter in this book, God's plan for your career.

In the first chapter I pointed out that this book dealt more with what you must "be" as a person instead of what you "do" in your job to reach your full potential. You see, when we talk about *managing to be the best,* we must clarify "who's best" we are talking about.

The real issue for managers has nothing to do with planning, leading, organizing, or controlling. It has nothing to do with decision-making skills, communication skills, team building skills, or time management skills. The most important issue faced by every manager is: *Will I be God's person, or "my" person.*

THE ISSUE OF "CONTROL"

All managers understand, and most seek and need, control. Management is all about the use of power and control. The further up the organizational ladder you climb, the more power and control you wield.

Striving for power and control is part of our human nature. We enjoy and thrive on being in charge. Being in charge allows us to be in control. And being in control is enormously satisfying to our egos.

However, I want to suggest that as long as you demand to control your own life you can never reach your full potential as a manager. That may shock some of you, and you may disagree. Many of you may have been taught, as I was, that you must be in control of your life to succeed.

We live in a self-centered world. We believe that no one is going to do it for us. To make it to the top we will have to do it ourselves. We think we have to look out for "number one," because no one else will. We grasp for power and control, because the more we have over our own lives the more we can succeed.

And to a certain extent that is all true. The harder we work at succeeding, the more successful we are likely to become. You may even accomplish every career goal you set for yourself, but that does not mean you have reached your full potential.

HOW IS POTENTIAL MEASURED?

Throughout this book I have frequently used the phrase, "reaching your full potential." What does that phrase mean to you? Do you think about being recognized as the best in your field? Do you think about being able to solve any management problem in the most effective way possible? Or maybe you're different. Maybe you think about finding that "perfect position" in some organization and simply living happily ever after.

What does reaching your full potential mean? Most of us think about achieving a certain position, making a certain amount of money, or reaching a certain level of recognition. All of these factors enter into the development of your full potential, but they are limited to a human perspective.

You see, God also has a view of your potential, and His view concerning your potential goes far beyond the comprehension of your small, finite, human mind. God wants to accomplish far greater things in and through you than you have ever imagined.

GOD HAS A PLAN FOR YOUR LIFE

The fact that God has a plan for our lives was one of the hardest issues I had to wrestle with after becoming a Christian. I could accept the fact that God created the universe, that He was all-powerful and all-knowing, and that He sent His Son to die on the cross for my sins. But I had a hard time accepting the idea that such a powerful God could be concerned with having a plan for *my* life.

Then I began to worry that if God really did have a plan for my life, maybe it wasn't as good a plan as I had, or maybe I wouldn't like the plan, so I wasn't so sure I really wanted to know what that plan was—if it existed at all.

God does have a plan for your life. Notice what God told Jeremiah: "The word of the Lord came to me, saying, 'Before I formed you in the womb I knew you, before you were born I set you apart; I appointed you as a prophet to the nations'" (Jer. 1:4-5, NIV). This verse points out that before Jeremiah was born God had already determined a plan for his life.

Jeremiah isn't the only example in the Bible of God having a plan for a person's life. Look at what God said to Abraham: "The Lord had said to Abram, 'Leave your country, your people, and your father's household and go to the land I will show you. I will make you into a great nation and I will bless you. I will make your name great, and you will be a blessing'" (Gen. 12:1-2, NIV). God had a plan to make Abraham the father of a great nation, and a part of that plan involved him moving out of the country of his birth.

Just as God had a specific plan for the lives of people in the Bible, he also has a specific plan for our lives today. Notice what Jeremiah 29:11 tells us: "'For I know the plans I have for you,' declares the Lord, 'plans to prosper you and not to harm you, plans to give you hope and a future'" (NIV).

God doesn't have a plan for some and not a plan for others. Just as God had a specific plan for Jeremiah He also has a specific plan for us today. The question is, are we willing to follow that plan.

We also have plans of our own. We have a life to live, things we want to do, hopes and dreams to pursue. And after all, how can we *really know* what God's plans for us are?

PREREQUISITE FOR KNOWING GOD'S PLANS FOR YOU

There are some prerequisites we must meet before we can know God's plans for us. I have never met a person who wasn't a Christian who knew God's plans. God doesn't waste His time communicating His plans to those who aren't willing to accept God and His authority in their lives.

Paul speaks to this issue. "Therefore, I urge you, brothers, in

168

view of God's mercy, to offer your bodies as living sacrifices, holy and pleasing to God—this is your spiritual worship. Do not conform any longer to the pattern of this world, but be transformed by the renewing of your mind. Then you will be able to test and approve what God's will is—His good, pleasing, and perfect will" (Rom. 12:1-2, NIV).

In these two verses we are given both the prerequisite for knowing God's plans for us and a description of those plans. First, we are told to offer our bodies as a "living sacrifice"; that is the prerequisite. However, what does it mean to be a living sacrifice? It means that I remove "self" from the throne of my life, from having control, and I allow God to reign.

This is what Paul was talking about when he said, "I have been crucified with Christ and I no longer live, but Christ lives in me" (Gal. 2:20, NIV). Paul had met the prerequisite as described in Romans 12:1-2. For you and I to know God's plan for us, we also must meet the prerequisite of "dying to self."

Once we meet the prerequisite described by Paul, we will be able to know what God's will is for us. We learn three things about God's will: it is good, pleasing, and perfect.

When God begins to reveal His plans (Rom. 12:2), we see that they are *good* plans, not bad. They are not only good, but they are *pleasing* to us. In fact, it says they are *perfect* plans. And isn't that what all of us are looking for, the perfect plan for our lives? However, we can only have God's perfect plan for our lives when we meet the prerequisites.

IDENTIFYING GOD'S PLANS FOR YOU

Once you've given control of your life and plans to God, then you are ready to begin identifying God's plans for you. Most of us tend to think God plays "hide and seek" with us. However, in reality, God is more interested in our knowing and doing His will than we are in finding it out and acting upon it.

Listen to Paul's words to the Philippians. "For it is God who is at work within you, giving you the will and the power to achieve His purpose" (Phil. 2:13, PH). This is a very important verse concerning God's plans for us. First, notice that God is going to work "within you." And that is why it is so important to meet the prerequisite of giving God control over your life.

The verse tells us that God works within us to do two things: to give us the *will* and the *power* to achieve His purpose and plans for our lives. Isn't that exciting? God says He will work directly in us, giving us the will to achieve His plans, and the power to accomplish them.

The question is, how does He work within us to achieve this? Psalm 37:4 gives us the answer: "Delight yourself in the LORD and He will give you the desires of your heart" (NIV). This verse gives us a condition and then a promise. The condition or prerequisite is to delight ourselves in the Lord. What does it mean to delight ourselves in the Lord? It means delighting in doing His will rather than ours.

Once we have done this, then we can claim the promise that God will give us the desires of our hearts. Because we are Christians, God will not give us every desire of our hearts. But as long as we are meeting the prerequisite of letting Him have control, then God may give us our desires.

According to Philippians 2:13, God is free to inject His will into us. He gives us "desires" to do His will. He gives us the desires of our heart as long as He has control of our wills. When He is in control, He is free to give us our desires because He has placed them there.

Of course, every desire is not from God. God never forces us to let Him stay in control. Just because we have a desire does not mean that it is from God.

So how can we know if a desire is from God? Remember, God not only gives the desire, He also provides the resources to achieve it. Therefore, if the desire is from God, the power needed to achieve it will be there. The resources will be available. If they aren't, one can conclude the following: either it isn't God's desire or, it may be His desire, but not the right timing.

However, let's assume we have the desire and the resources are also there. Does that prove that it is God's plan for us? Not necessarily; there is still one more "test" in determining God's plan.

Look at what Isaiah 26:3 says, "You will keep in perfect peace him whose mind is steadfast, because he trusts in You" (NIV). God promises that as long as our minds are trusting in Him we will have peace. Thus, if you begin acting on a desire, but God does not give you peace about it as you seek His guidance, then you know that desire is not from Him.

Knowing God's Plan for Your Life

Let's summarize the process of knowing God's plans for us:
1. Recognize the fact that God does have a plan for your life (Jer. 1:4-5).
2. Meet the prerequisite of giving God control over your will (Rom. 12:1-2; Gal. 2:20).
3. Recognize God is working within you to give you the desire and power to accomplish His plans (Ps. 37:4; Phil. 2:13).
4. Begin acting on those desires and watch for the power and resources to achieve those plans (Phil. 2:13).
5. If the power and resources are not available, or don't become available, assume the desire was not of God, or else it is not the right time (Phil. 2:13).
6. If the power and resources are there to achieve the desire, then check to see if God gives you peace to continue pursuing the plans (Isa. 26:3).

GOD'S PLANS: BAD TIMES AS WELL AS GOOD

Many think that God's plans for us always consist of good times. That is not true. Yes, as Romans 12:2 points out, God's plans for us are "good, acceptable, and perfect." But that does not mean that if we are going through hard times we are necessarily outside of God's plans for us.

Notice what Deuteronomy 8:2 tells us. "Remember how the Lord your God led you all the way in the desert these forty years, to humble you and to test you in order to know what was in your heart, whether or not you would keep His commands" (NIV). God led the entire nation of Israel, with all of their flocks and herds, directly into the desert. God's plan for the people was the desert!

Just as God's plan for the Children of Israel included the desert, His plan for your life will also include trips through dry times. And it is the trials and problems in our lives that God uses to develop us into mature, complete people. Notice what James says: "Dear brothers, is your life full of difficulties and temptations? Then be happy, for when the way is rough, your patience has a chance to grow. So let it grow, and don't try to squirm out of your problems. For when your patience is finally in full bloom, then you will be ready for anything, strong in character, full, and complete" (James 1:2-4, TLB).

God uses problems and difficulties to help mold us into mature people with more potential for accomplishing the great plans He has for us. That is why we should take a positive approach to our problems. It is the setbacks in life that help develop us into stronger people.

Yes, there will be problems in life. Some of those problems are a part of God's master plan for us. The psalmist offers insight here, "What I [God] want from you is your true thanks; I want your promises fulfilled. *I want you to trust Me in your times of trouble, so I can rescue you, and you can give Me glory*" (Ps. 50:15, TLB). God promises that for every problem we have He has the power needed to rescue us. We are simply to give Him the credit for solving the problems instead of taking the credit ourselves.

HOW GOD WANTS TO USE YOUR CAREER

We have seen that God does, in fact, have a plan for each of our lives. God not only has a plan, He promises to reveal that plan to us. "I will instruct you and teach you in the way you should go; I will counsel you and watch over you" (Ps. 32:8, NIV). That is a great promise of God.

The Bible also tells us other things about God's plans for us. Jesus said, "You are the light of the world. A city on a hill cannot be hidden. Neither do people light a lamp and put it under a bowl. Instead they put it on its stand, and it gives light to everyone in the house. In the same way, let your light shine before men, that they may see your good deeds and praise your Father in heaven" (Matt. 5:14-16, NIV).

Notice this passage doesn't say we should do this only if we feel "called to the ministry." We are all "called" to be witnesses of

Jesus Christ, to be lights in a dark world. We are to work at reaching people and building up the body of Christ. God's plan is for all of us to be "full-time workers" in building up His kingdom. He calls some of us to be pastors and others to be managers, teachers, and doctors. But the call is all the same. Therefore, as a manager, part of God's plan for your career is that you be a light in your business pointing the way, by your words and deeds, to Jesus.

Your life is a witness either for or against God. You can't be neutral. God's plan is that you be an effective witness for Him in your career. According to Matthew 4:19 we are all called to be fishing for people—some of us as managers, some as bus drivers, some as engineers, some as students. But no matter what God's plan for our lives, we know it will involve reaching out to people and helping them find a personal relationship with Jesus Christ.

THE WAR IN THE MARKETPLACES OF THE WORLD

I travel all over the world meeting with people in the marketplace. During the past few years God seems to be raising up Christian managers and businesspeople, in every country, who realize the need to use their careers as a strong witness for Jesus Christ. "Lay" people in the marketplaces of the world are seeing their obligation to serve God in and through their jobs as never before. God is using the "layman" to impact the marketplace with the Gospel, and as a result, many people are coming to Christ.

Career people, in all walks of life, are recognizing that God wants to use them and their careers to help reach the world. And what better way to serve as a witness than among those you work with every day. Small group Bible studies are springing up during lunch hours all over the world. Managers and businesspeople are meeting together in early-morning Bible studies to learn to be more effective in taking the Gospel to their peers.

God wants to use you and your management career, not just to provide for your family's needs, but as powerful and effective witness to your fellow managers, subordinates, and peers in the workplace. And God promises unlimited power available to back those who will get involved in accomplishing this aspect of His worldwide plan.

Let me ask again what the phrase, *reaching your full potential as a manager,* means to you. I have used it throughout this book. We have talked about decisions you must make and what you need to "be" as a person to successfully climb the organizational ladder. But if your definition of reaching your potential centers around climbing ladders and accumulating wealth, you are settling for second best.

No matter how successful you become according to the standards of this world, someday you will die and leave it all behind, and someone else will enjoy the fruits of all your labor. In Matthew 5:19 we are encouraged to focus on storing up treasures in heaven instead of earth, because the treasures in heaven are eternal.

You need to invest your efforts in things that are of eternal value, not simply material value. You will never reach and experience your full potential focusing on material things. To be all that God intended you to be, you must focus your attention on things of eternal value.

In Mark 16:15 we are told, "Go into all the world and preach the good news to all creation" (NIV). That is as much a part of our job as the day-to-day functions of management. In fact, it is our job while performing the day-to-day functions as a manager. God is counting on managers in the marketplace to be faithful in sharing the good news of the Gospel, because the war for control of the marketplace will be won or lost according to our obedience.

WHAT ARE YOU WORTH TO GOD?

What are you worth to God? Understanding the answer to that question forever changed the direction of my life. Notice the questions Jesus asked, "What good will it be for a man if he gains the whole world, yet forfeits his soul? Or what can a man give in exchange for his soul?" (Matt. 16:26, NIV)

These are powerfully sobering questions. I have traveled throughout a good part of the world. I have seen the vast resources accumulated by the world's largest businesses. But notice what Jesus is saying. All the world's riches don't begin to equal the value of just one soul. That is how much you are worth to God.

That is why He willingly gave His Son that you and I might have eternal life. If a person is worth that much to God, shouldn't we begin looking at our potential from the standpoint of not how much we can acquire, but how much we can give for the sake of the Gospel. That is where our real potential is experienced! If we set that priority, we will be *managing to be the best.*

PERSONAL APPLICATION

1. What was your purpose and objective in reading this book? How has this book influenced your thinking on developing your potential as a manager?
2. Who is in control of your life and plans—you or God?
3. What have you learned in this chapter about the importance of letting God have control of your life?
4. What impact will it have on our lives when we let God be in control?
5. Is there more potential when we are in control, or when God is in control? Explain.
6. How do we give God control of our lives? What is the result?
7. How can you let God more effectively use your career as a light in the marketplace? (see Matt. 4:19; 5:14-16)